GREAT PUZZLES OF HISTORY

GREAT PUZZLES OF HISTORY

INTRIGUING CASES OF THE PAST

Fred Neff

RP RUNESTONE PRESS • MINNEAPOLIS

Acknowledgments

All photos copyrighted to and reproduced with the permission of:
Archive Photos, pp. 11, 19, 35, 43, 53, 74, 93; Corbis-Bettmann, p. 65.

Cover photo/p. 83 courtesy of Archive Photos.

Runestone Press
A division of Lerner Publications Company
241 First Avenue North
Minneapolis, MN 55401

Library of Congress Cataloging-in-Publication Data

Neff, Fred.
    Great puzzles of history : intriguing cases of the past / by Fred Neff.
      p.   cm.
    Includes bibliographical references.
    Summary: Presents discussions of ten historical controversies,
including the fate of Marie Antoinette's son, the true identity of
Prisoner Number 7 (Rudolf Hess), the existence of King Arthur, and
the discovery of America.
    ISBN 0-8225-3931-4 (alk. paper)
    1. World history—Miscellanea—Juvenile literature. [1. World
history—Miscellanea.] I. Title.
D21.3.N43 1997
909.08—dc21   96-50925

Manufactured in the United States of America
1 2 3 4 5 6 – JR – 02 01 00 99 98 97

This book is dedicated to the following family and friends who have so unwaveringly shown their confidence in me and their support for this book:

Christa Neff
Mollie Neff
Scott Neff
Theresa Freeman
Margaret McCoy
Michael Gaughan, Jr.
Richard DeValerio
James Reid
John Krezowski

Contents

Introduction

Despite the fact that the twentieth century is drawing to a close, there are still numerous unanswered questions about our history and the world around us. These baffling matters are puzzles of history that may never be solved, but the process of researching, studying and trying to solve them is rewarding. Even if no definitive answer can be reached the study of such colorful historical mysteries is entertaining, educational and stretches the imagination. The topics that have been selected for this book on Great Puzzles of History have been selected because they are historically significant and have a mystery surrounding them, which has made them controversial. Each of the topics have interesting and intriguing twists that allow for more than one interpretation of what happened or why something was done. This allows the reader a chance to historically interpret the events in light of his or her own judgment. In the process of doing this the reader may enjoy the role of detective by gathering facts, analyzing them, synthesizing the various facts and then drawing conclusions that can act as a basis for his or her own judgment. This type of critical thinking can only be developed by practice and is of great use in everyday life.

1

The Lost Dauphin

In the Temple prison in France in July of 1793, a young mother was startled by the entry of several men into her cell, who announced that they were going to be taking her 8-year-old son away. Her pleas and sobs to keep the child were to no avail. The heartbroken mother was Marie Antoinette, the once haughty wife of King Louis XVI of France. The French Revolution that started in 1789, not only swept away the grandeur of her husband's rule, but the fabric of her life. Earlier in the year, on January 21, 1793, King Louis XVI, or Citizen Capet as he was commonly referred to by the revolutionaries, was found guilty of treason, and guillotined. The Queen's miserable existence was not to extend much longer, for she was executed herself in October, 1793. Although the major events of the French Revolution have been well docu-

Louis XVII of France, the Lost Dauphin

mented, there still remains the enduring mystery of the final fate of the young prince.

After the Dauphin was taken away from his mother, he was placed in another room elsewhere in the Temple prison. A cobbler, Antoine Simon, was assigned to act as a tutor to the prince. It was hoped that young Louis Charles would be flexible enough to adapt to what was required of a child of the revolution. He was taught to drink, swear, and behave as would be expected of an enemy of the aristocracy. Louis Charles was even coached or possibly forced into making charges against his own mother, which were used at the trial that led to her execution. The cobbler and his wife were not interested in adopting Louis Charles as their own son. Their goal was to train him in revolutionary dogma. The young Dauphin got attention from them, but not love. By January of 1794, the Simons left their posts as mentors to the young prince. Did the tutors quit because they did not like the manipulative treatment of the child or did the revolutionary leaders decide that it did not look appropriate for the former prince to be given the special privilege of a tutor?

Once the Simons no longer looked after the young prince, he was forced to live a very lonely and depressing lifestyle. His world was a room with a grill on the door where he was watched by his jailers. As the days of his captivity rolled on, the room became dirtier and the living conditions more squalid. After a while, it seemed as though the prince had lost the will to live because he seemed to show very little emotion. His physical condition deteriorated, and he was developing signs of rickets. There was swelling and deformity around the area of the joints in his legs. Despite the fact that his physical health was deteriorating, no help was forthcoming in 1794. Finally, in May of 1795, Dr. Desault, who was a renowned physician in Paris, came to make an examination of the child.

The doctor was upset when he left from his visit with the child, causing speculation since then about what had caused him such great concern. Was the doctor concerned with the treatment of the child or did he question the identity of the person he examined? After his visit, Dr. Desault requested that the boy be removed to a living space where there was better light and ventilation. His request was not honored. Dr. Desault died mysteriously within a short time of his visit with the prince. There was a rumor that the doctor's widow had hinted that he had refused to take part in an unusual plan involving the child in the cell. Was Dr. Desault killed because he refused to be a party to the murder of the young prince?

The leaders of the Revolution were not the only people who took a tremendous interest in young Louis Charles. The Royalists, who still supported the idea that France should be ruled by a king, had not forgotten about the prince. They wanted to destroy the Revolution and once more put a king upon the throne. Could the Royalists have killed Dr. Desault because his examination revealed the possibility that Louis Charles earlier had been removed from the cell and that another child had been substituted in his place? The person in the cell, who was allegedly the French Dauphin, finally ended his torturous existence shortly after the examination of Dr. Desault. On June 8, 1795, the Dauphin died.

When a post mortem was conducted, it was the conclusion of the doctors that the person in the cell had died from a tubercular condition. Later the alleged corpse of the Dauphin was put in a coffin and buried in a common grave. Rumors spread like wildfire throughout France that the Dauphin had not been the person who was buried. The royal child supposedly had been earlier taken out of the Temple prison. Another child who was deaf and dumb had replaced him in the cell.

The doctors who examined the corpse found in the cell had never made a finding that the body that they examined belonged to Louis Charles. They instead centered their inquiry into the causes of the death of the corpse that they were examining. When the coffin was later exhumed in 1846, the skeleton in it did nothing to wash away the mystery of what happened to the Dauphin. The skull had a wisdom tooth in it and the limbs seemed too long for a young boy. Could the corpse have been that of a person in his later teenage years?

If the Royalists liberated Louis Charles from his prison cell, then why didn't they publicly claim their successful plot and move to put him on the throne? Although the prince may have been helped through a successful plan to escape the terrible fate in the cell, there may have been a later decision that he was not the best person to represent the aristocracy as a king. The prince was rumored to have been of delicate physical condition even in his confinement. He probably would not have been strong enough to fulfill his royal duties by the spring of 1795. If he had survived, Louis Charles might not have wanted to physically take up the challenges necessary to try and become king.

As the years passed, a number of people came forward to claim that they were the Dauphin. It is estimated that there were approximately forty pretenders to the French throne. The vast majority of people claiming to be Louis Charles lacked sufficient evidence to prove their claim and were soon publicly discredited.

Among the proposed candidates who allegedly could have been the Dauphin was none other than the famous naturalist, John James Audubon. The famous artist, who contributed greatly to the study of American birds, started out life according to some recordings as the illegitimate son of a French naval officer. There have been questions about Audubon's origins which have never been cleared up, since no certificate of Audubon's birth was allegedly available for review. Some people have doubted the claim that he was born in Santo Domingo, on April 26, 1785. This date of birth is, however, close to the birth of Louis Charles on March 27, 1785. Audubon was supposedly adopted on March 7, 1794, which would be around two months after the Dauphin's tutor, Antoine Simon, left the Temple prison. Could the Dauphin have been rescued from his cell and snuck out of France for adoption?

Audubon supposedly explained to his family that he had felt funny visiting Paris in 1828, as an ordinary tourist, since he earlier had been destined for such a special role in life. Nevertheless, neither Audubon nor his heirs ever made a formal claim to the French throne.

Probably the most effective of the claimants to being the Dauphin was a German clockmaker by the name of Karl Wihelm Naundorff. He traveled to Paris in 1833 to assert his right of birth. The Dauphin's childhood nurse, Madam de Rambaud, observed that Naundorff greatly resembled what she remembered of the child, Louis

Charles, before the revolution. The claimant even appeared to have scars and birthmarks that resembled ones observed on the Dauphin. Naundorff also displayed knowledge of the Dauphin's early years at court. The physical evidence and the special knowledge displayed by Naundorff won him support from backers throughout France. In 1836, he followed up his claim with a formal suit for a recovery of the property of the Dauphin. Naundorff was never able to formally present his position at a trial. Instead, the government arrested and deported him. Did the King of France fear that Naundorff could produce sufficient evidence to support his claim to being the legitimate heir to the French throne? On more than one occasion Naundorff was assaulted with deadly force. Could the assaults have been unsuccessful attempts at murdering the real heir to the French throne?

After leaving France, Naundorff's travels eventually took him to the Netherlands. He settled down there to work on mechanical repair projects and clock work. Eventually, he developed a design for a new weapon that was purchased by the Dutch government. When he died in 1845, his tombstone appeared to signify that he was recognized by some people as Louis XVII, which would have made him a member of the select group that are recognized as French kings. Naundorff's death did not end the controversy as to his identity. Periodically, his heirs faced challenges to the claim that Naundorff was a part of the royal family of France.

The mystery that surrounds the disappearance of the lost Dauphin will remain a part of the heritage of the turmoil that came out of the French Revolution.

2

The Anastasia Controversy

A young woman looked down into the murky water below as she poised herself on the edge of the bridge across the Landwehr Canal in Berlin, Germany, in February of 1920. A policeman standing nearby observed her jump into the icy waters. After a dramatic rescue by him, the young woman was taken to a hospital for treatment. The search for her true identity was to take on worldwide proportions and spawn one of the great civil lawsuits in history.

At the hospital, it was observed that the woman appeared to be twenty years of age, but had no papers or written identification that would give a clue as to her name or origin. She was in very poor medical condition and seemed either unable or unwilling to respond to questions. The patient's continued failure to supply information about herself led to her being transferred to the Dalldorf asylum for possible assistance with mental illness. At the asylum, she was commonly known as "Miss Unknown." An examination of her body revealed that she had distinctive scars, deformities, and damage to her upper jaw. Her body appeared as if it had possibly been severely beaten in the past. Scars gave an indication that she may have been stabbed and even shot. It was not clear where the unknown woman was originally born. She spoke German with an accent that indicated she was raised in another country. It was observed, however, that she communicated and carried herself as though she was born to a royal family. One inmate at the asylum thought Ms. Unknown resembled one of the daughters of the last Czar of Russia, who had allegedly been killed after the Russian Revolution.

In the days that followed the announcement of the slaughter of the Russian imperial family at Ekaterinburg in July of 1918, rumors spread that some of the Czar's family may have escaped death. At the asylum there was speculation that Ms. Unknown could be one of the members of the imperial Russian family that escaped death at the hands of the Bolsheviks. Finally in the fall of 1921, Ms. Unknown revealed that she was really the Grand Duchess, Anastasia Nikolaevna, the youngest daughter of Nicholas II, the last Czar of Russia. Word filtered out to the Russians living in Berlin that one of the imperial Russian family was alive. A Russian emigré, Baron Von Kleist, met with the claimant and invited her to stay at his home in 1922. She was still ill and subject to relapses where she became physically unable to handle even ordinary conversation. Despite her weak medical condition, the former mental patient was subjected to a great deal of questioning while living with the Baron's family.

Grand Duchess Anastasia

Russians traveled to see the woman who called herself Anastasia. Although the claimant had shown knowledge of the imperial family in discussions with Baron Von Kleist, she was not always able to display her knowledge to visitors. Was she unable to handle the interviews because of her physical condition or to cover up the fact she was incapable of proving her claim?

Some people felt insulted and resentful after meeting with the woman who claimed to be a daughter of the last Russian imperial ruler. Her uncooperative attitude and demeanor lost her key support. There began to be rumors that Baron Von Kleist fed information to the claimant who was a pretender to being the youngest daughter of Czar Nicholas II. It was said that he hoped to receive a financial profit if she was recognized. The Czar's daughter would be open to inheriting whatever financial interests the Russian ruler had left after the revolution in his country. Supposedly, the Czar had millions of dollars on deposit in German and English banks.

The Baron was able to convince some people that Anastasia was difficult because of her poor medical condition. This did not explain her failure, however, to give a clear narration of her survival at Ekaterinberg when the rest of the imperial family allegedly died there. The Baron and other supporters of the claimant supposedly pieced together the sketchy and incoherent information related to them by her to elucidate why she was able to survive the Bolshevik slaughter. They explained that she had been present when the Bolshevik soldiers came down to the basement at the Villa Ipatiev mansion to kill the Czar's family on July of 1918. The soldiers' shots hit the rest of Anastasia's family. Her sister, Tatiana's, body fell, however, in such a way as to shield her. The last thing she remembered of that night was a violent blow on the head that caused her to pass out. She was later taken in a wagon across country. During that time, she was quite ill, having experienced serious wounds to her head and body. Her rescuers were named Tchaikovski. She was smuggled out of Ekaterinberg by Alexander Tchaikovski in an effort to save her life.

Finally, she ended up in Bucharest where she lived for some time as the wife of one of the Tschaikovskis. During that time, the jewelry that had been secretly sewn into her clothing was slowly sold off to pay for her living expenses. A son was born to Anastasia in 1919 out of the relationship with Tchaikovski. Her husband was later killed and her baby taken away from her. The implication was that the assassination and taking of the child were related to a Bolshevik conspiracy against a member of the former Russian imperial family. Anastasia then traveled to Germany to escape the Bolsheviks. When her travel companion disappeared, she felt like giving up and jumped into the canal.

Attempts were made to gather evidence to support Anastasia's story. A former communications officer came forward to state that he recalled some peasants waiting to cross the bridge in the area described by her. At the time, he had been told that the cart contained the Czar's youngest daughter Anastasia. Another person recalled being in a jewelry shop when a valuable pearl necklace from Russia was brought in by a person that could have been Alexander Tchaikovski.

Despite Anastasia's knowledge of the Russian imperial family, possible physical resemblance with the

21

members of the Czar's family, explanation of survival, and supporting witnesses, there were still nagging suspicions about her. For one thing, she continued to communicate in German and steadfastly refused to speak Russian. Some people questioned whether she was really born in Russia, let alone a daughter of Czar Nicholas II.

The answer to her claim, some people felt, was in the report of an investigator for the counter revolutionaries, Nicholas Sokolov, who had examined the scene of the alleged murder of the Czar's family in January of 1919. His report contained evidence that indicated that everyone in the Czar's family, including the family dog, had been killed. He theorized that the family's bodies had first been burnt. Later the remaining fragments of the family's bodies were then subjected to acid. What was left after flame and acid was deposited in a nearby mine along with some of their possessions. Sokolov even had witnesses that claimed to know that the imperial family and their immediate servants were murdered in July of 1918 at Ekaterinberg.

The woman who was fished out of the canal in Berlin in 1920 was not the only person who claimed to have survived the slaughter at Ekaterinberg. Other claimants stated that they were surviving members of the Czar's family. It seemed to many people that there was nothing special that made the woman from Dalldorf asylum stand apart from the other claimants, except her uncooperative attitude. Her detractors made a great deal out of the fact that the real Grand Duchess, Anastasia, as a young woman had the ability to speak English, German, Russian, and even French. They reasoned that if the woman who was now claiming to be Anastasia was a true Romanov, she would be willing to speak in these languages.

Could Anastasia have had the ability to speak Russian, but not want to do it on command? The Bolshevik guards allegedly abused the Czar's captive family. In the process of controlling the imperial family, they forced them to speak Russian. Could Anastasia's failure to speak Russian be a reaction to past pressure by her cruel Bolshevik captors? If Anastasia was a fake, wouldn't she have learned Russian and made it a point to speak it to support her claim?

The fact that key relatives of the last Czar, such as Prussian crowned Princess Cecile and Princess Irena of Prussia, who was the sister of the Czarina, failed to accept her claim seriously weakened her bid for recognition. The last Czar's mother, the Dowager Empress, Marie Fedorovna, refused to accept that her son and his family had died at Ekaterinberg. The Empress was of the opinion that her son's family all remained in hiding together. She could not accept that one member of the family had been separated from the others. She viewed Anastasia as an imposter.

Anastasia's supporters argued that the horrors that she had been put through by the Bolsheviks had obviously affected her emotionally. They believed that she should not be judged by her behavior, but rather the physical evidence that supported her claims. It was known that the Grand Duchess Anastasia had injured one finger of her left hand as a child. The left hand of the claimant had the same type of injury. The shoulder of the Grand Duchess Anastasia had been cauterized when she was young and the woman who claimed to be her exhibited the type of scar that would be expected after such a procedure. One of the distinctive things about the youngest imperial Duchess had been the bunions on her feet. The woman known as Anastasia during the 1920s exhibited the same type of physical deformity. Experts in judging physical characteristics of the human body were called into the case. Photographs were taken of identifying marks on the claimant's body. A plaster cast was even made of her deformed toe joint. This evidence was presented to the Grand Duke Ernst Ludwig of Hess, who was Anastasia's uncle. His opinion carried considerable weight with both the German and Russian aristocracy. He remained unimpressed with the evidence shown him and refused to accept the claimant.

It was arranged for the tutor of the Czar's family, Pierre Geillard, to meet with Anastasia. Both he and his wife, who had been Anastasia's nurse, came to meet her. The meeting did not produce the kind of results that Anastasia's supporters had expected. Later, Pierre Geillard came out with a public statement that Anastasia was an imposter. The claimant was, however, recognized by some other people who had possibly known the real Grand Duchess better than the former tutor. Gleb Botken, who was the son of the Czar's personal physician, remained one of Anastasia's most steadfast supporters. He and others like him argued that she was truly the last Czar's daughter.

There were charges that Geillard had been influenced by the Grand Duke Ernst Ludwig of Hess in making his opinion. Some people believed that the Grand Duke Ernst Ludwig of Hess pressured others to side against the claimant. Why would the Grand Duke be so adamant in not accepting Anastasia's claim?

Anastasia had earlier stated the Grand Duke, who was formerly a German general, had come to visit her father during World War I in Russia. If the Grand Duke tried to make a separate peace with the Czar during the war, then his loyalty to Germany would be open to attack. Ernst Ludwig of Hess publicly refuted ever having visited with Czar Nicholas II during World War I. It seemed that for him to accept Anastasia as the rightful heir, he would also have to acknowledge that she was correct in stating he had visited with the Czar during the war. Was his privileged status in Germany fragile enough that he feared putting himself in a position where his loyalty and patriotism were in question? Did the Grand Duke Ernst not recognize Anastasia because he wanted to make a claim for his relatives to what was left of the Czar's wealth?

Although there was a great deal of interest in what was left of the Czar's wealth after his death, no large amount of Russian Imperial assets were ever found in either Germany or in England. Unfortunately for Anastasia, it was not until many years later, after the Grand Duke Hess and his followers had done a great deal of damage to her cause that more than one source allegedly revealed that the Grand Duke Ernst Ludwig of Hess, had visited Russia during World War I. Possibly, he may have been sent on a secret mission by the German Kaiser, who was a relative of the Czar's wife, in an attempt to get a separate peace with the Russians so that Germans could concentrate their energies on fighting against the other allied forces.

There were even detractors who tried to prove that the claimant was not of Russian noble birth, but instead a Polish peasant by the name of Franziska Schanzkovsky.

Franziska's relatives, however, never made a positive identification of the claimant as a part of their family.

In February of 1928, Anastasia set sail to America to visit with Princess Xenia, who was of Russian descent. While in the United States, she went by the name of Anna Anderson. The use of this name came back to haunt her in later years. Some people argued that this was an open acknowledgment that she was not Anastasia and that her real name was Anna Anderson.

Even while visiting with Princess Xenia, Anastasia remained difficult to communicate with about her past. Although she won over new converts to her cause, there were other people who were turned off by her behavior. Anastasia continued to take the position that it was not necessary for her to prove her identity. She was encouraged in the 1930s to apply for a cancellation of the German court decision that the imperial family was dead and that the last Czar's German possessions were to pass to his secondary heirs. The litigation continued for many years.

In 1938 a person by the name of Franz Svoboda, who was an Austrian prisoner of war in 1918, made a statement that after the massacre at the Ipatiev mansion a girl was still moving. He recalled helping to take the girl to a nearby house. There were also claims that the Russian police had even posted notices over the Ekaterinberg area after July of 1918 stating that a female member of the imperial family had been abducted. Supposedly, the Bolsheviks had even searched houses and trains looking for the missing family member.

The coming of World War II and the chaotic years that followed disrupted a court decision on the controversy.

Experts were, however, secured to review the evidence in preparation for the eventual trial. It was found that there was a match when pictures and measurements of the real Grand Duchess were compared with the physical characteristics of the claimant. Similarly, handwriting experts found that a comparison of the writing of the real Grand Duchess as a young woman and Anna Anderson proved that they were the same person. It wasn't until the middle of the 1950s that the controversy proceeded to trial. The German court followed strict procedures that some people felt were unfair to the claimant. After reviewing the evidence, the court decided that Anna Anderson had not proven that she was the Grand Duchess Anastasia. The decision was appealed by her.

In 1968, Anna married a history professor by the name of John Manahand. Until the end of her life, he remained a staunch supporter of her claim to being the Grand Duchess Anastasia. After years of legal fighting, the West German Supreme Court finally decided to reject Ms. Anderson's plea. Their decision was not so much a rejection of her identity, but an acceptance that the lower court's procedures had been correct. The final court decision merely left the impression that the claimant had not fully proven her claim. There was no finding by the court that the claimant, Anna Anderson, was someone other than the Grand Duchess Anastasia.

In spite of the West German Supreme Court's rejection of her plea for recognition, Anna Anderson continued to win supporters for her cause. Supporters of Anna Anderson's claim to being Anastasia argued that there was never substantial evidence to prove that the whole imperial family of Russia was slaughtered at the Villa

27

Ipatiev in July of 1918. To the contrary, there was evidence of sightings of Romanovs elsewhere in Russia after the alleged murders. One doctor even testified that he was taken by Bolshevik agents to treat a woman that they claimed was the last Czar's daughter months after the alleged murder of the imperial family.

Sokolov's claim that the dead Czar's family and servants' remains and possessions were found in the mine did not ring true to everyone. Would fire and acid destroy a human body to the extent that there would be very little left of the skeletal remains? No complete skeleton of the family was ever found in the mine. Yet, the decimated remains of the family's dog allegedly turned up in the mine. It seems strange that the dog's body was in such good condition almost a year after the alleged murder, while the human remains were incomplete and unrecognizable. The remnants of a finger found in the mine that allegedly was from the Czar's wife also seemed suspicious. Why would a part of the finger remain while the rest of the body was destroyed? Why were so few possessions of the imperial family found by the investigators? Could the mines have been salted with false evidence by the Bolsheviks in order to convince opposing forces in support of the Czar to believe that the former ruler's family had been killed? Could the Bolsheviks have kept the Czar's family in hiding, hoping that they could use them for ransom to trade with the German Kaiser? It was known that the German Kaiser felt an affinity to his relative the Czarina and that he wanted to keep her family safe.

If the Romanov family survived, then why were they not eventually revealed to the world? The explanation that has been accepted by some of Anna Anderson's sup-porters is that the Czar may have been killed in July of 1918, but the Czarina and her daughters were spared. When the Bolsheviks later changed their decision to use the imperial family as hostages for trade, they were killed. Anastasia may not have escaped from the tradi-tional murder scene at the Ipatiev mansion, but instead later ran away from a place her family had been moved to after July of 1918. Possibly, she felt guilty for having left her mother and sisters in the hands of the Bolshe-viks who later murdered them. Supposedly, Anna Ander-son had claimed that she could never tell the whole story. Was she unwilling to tell her story because of guilt for leaving her mother and sisters alone? Could she have accepted the Baron's version because it relieved her of the stigma of disloyalty in leaving her mother and sisters in the deadly grasp of the Bolsheviks?

The death of Anna Anderson in 1984 only served to fan the flames of controversy over her true identity. In the early 1990s the secrets of the Kremlin began to emerge from the Soviet government archives. After the loss of tight communist control over information related to the Czar and his family's death, the archival material cast doubt on the officially accepted version of the death of the Czar's family.

In 1991, in the Ekaterinburg area the skeletal remains of what many believe are the Czar's family were exhumed. The grave site was allegedly known for some time previ-ous to 1991, but unable to be publicly revealed because of the communist power structure in the former Soviet Union. Two of the Czar's family seemed to be missing. A controversy broke out as to whether Anastasia's skeleton was among those found. Portions of the Ekaterinburg skeletons underwent DNA analysis. The conclusion was that the DNA pattern of the tested material appeared to be the same as members of the royal family. A small portion of Anna Anderson's tissue left over from an operation was tested, but did not appear to match the DNA pattern of the skeletons.

Anna Anderson's supporters refused to accept that the results show she was not Anastasia and point out that recent forensic comparisons of her face and ears show that they match that of Anastasia. Some of these same supporters still question the authenticity and accuracy of the identification of the skeletal remains and the alleged tissue of Anna Anderson used for testing. Possibly, it will never be known for sure whether or not Anna Anderson was the last Czar's daughter, but to some people she remains an example of a lost period of time and with storybook beauty and nobility that they wish to recapture.

3

The Missing English Princes

A wooden chest containing the skeletons of two children was discovered in the Tower of London by a workman in July of 1674. Ever since that time there has been speculation over whose remains were found in the tower. Some people believe the skeletons were what is left of two missing English princes known to history as Richard Duke of York and the uncrowned King Edward V. The royal youngsters disappeared behind a curtain of mystery that was spun out of the political intrigue of late fifteenth century England.

Is there a connection between the lost English princes and the bones found in the tower? To try and find the answer it is necessary to review what it was like in England during the last half of the fifteenth century.

Civil war raged on and off in England from 1455 to

1471 in the conflict that is known as the War of the Roses. Two great families called the House of Lancaster and the House of York fought one another for the right to have their representative become ruler of England. Political power seesawed from one influential family to the other. The English people were caught between the two families who were striving for the right to rule England.

After the battle of Mortimer's Cross, Edward IV was accepted as the new King of England. Unlike some of his predecessors, he was extremely handsome, forceful, and had the demeanor of a king. He came into power with a wave of popularity. At the time, it was widely accepted that the twenty-three year old king was a bachelor. He later, however, shocked the public by announcing that he was married to Lady Elizabeth Grey, who was the widow of a Lancastrian knight. Lady Grey had a son from a previous marriage and was 4 years older than Edward IV. Although many people felt that it was an unfortunate marriage, they accepted the union because nothing could be done to change it. Edward and Elizabeth had children during their marriage. When Edward died in 1483, it came as a great blow both to his family and to England. Richard of Gloucester, who was Edward's brother, was given the title of protector with the right to govern England until his nephew came of age. It did not seem unusual for Gloucester to rule while young King Edward, who was only twelve and a half years old at the time, was prepared for office. Unfortunately, the arrangement did not take into account the protector's animosity toward the Queen's family and his own ambition to rule.

Richard of Gloucester was a man who would exert force when necessary to achieve his goal. As a young man, he had fought with valor in the War of the Roses. He continued to vigorously support his brother King Edward IV. It has been rumored, however, that Richard had a sinister side to his nature. He was even accused of murdering his own brother, George, and the deposed Lancastrian King, Henry VI, who had preceded his older brother as ruler of England. It seemed that people who knew Richard of Gloucester looked at him with suspicion while maintaining admiration for his brother Edward. It may be unfair to blame Richard alone for the murder of Henry VI when it was Edward IV who would have directly benefited from his predecessor's removal. Did Edward order Richard to perform the murder?

Given Richard of Gloucester's desire to rule, taste for power, and hatred for his sister-in-law, it seemed inevitable that they would clash. After King Edward IV died, the major barrier to Gloucester assuming full control over England as king were his two young nephews, Edward and Richard. Although young Edward was generally accepted to be king, he had not gone through a formal coronation. Before Edward could be brought to the coronation, two relatives of his who were strong supporters were arrested. His mother, sensing that she might be next, fled to Westminster Abbey with her younger children for sanctuary. While there, she learned that her brother and son by an earlier marriage were executed. It seemed that Gloucester was now accusing her of exercising witchcraft.

King Edward and his younger brother, Richard, Duke of York, were placed in the Tower of London. The coronation of Edward was now moved from May to June. Later, the story was that the coronation was going to be moved from June to November. As June of 1483 rolled around, it became publicly known that a bishop had determined that all the children born out of the relationship between King Edward IV and Elizabeth Woodville (Grey) were illegitimate. The bishop's reasoning was that Edward IV had allegedly made a contract to marry another woman before the children's births. After Gloucester took on his new role as king, the two royal children in the tower quickly faded from public view. They were last seen publicly in July playing in the gardens of the Tower. The rumor spread in the summer of 1483 that Richard had ordered that his nephews be executed.

Richard's rule was not to prove to be long or glorious. At the Battle of Bosworth Field he was defeated by a man who was later crowned Henry VII. The winner at Bosworth was at least as strong-willed, determined, and ambitious as Richard. He was to establish his own successful line of kings that are known as the Tudors. Under the rule of the Tudor monarchs there was speculation over what actually happened to the young boys who had been placed in the Tower in 1483. The illustrious Sir Thomas More was instrumental in developing the widely accepted version that a Sir James Tyrell had been retained by Richard III to help engineer the murder of the princes. In order to accomplish this, he in turn hired two thugs by the names of Forest and Dighton. Their job was to smother the children while they were in bed and to hide their corpses by burying them at the foot of the stairs in the tower. The children's remains were later supposedly moved to a more respectable and well accepted burial place. The great playwright, Shakespeare, popularized the story of Richard III's cruel murder of his nephews. Under

*This drawing shows Richard Duke of York and Edward V (in the
bed) about to be killed in the Tower of London.*

Shakespeare's pen, Richard turned from an ambitious noble who was an able administrator to a terrible monster who took the throne at the expense of his own nephews.

Shakespeare's view has not, however, been accepted by everyone who has studied the events that took place in the later half of the fifteenth century. His plays were written at a time when England was ruled by a Tudor. In the reign of Queen Elizabeth I, it would have been prudent for a playwright to depict Richard as being wicked. By making him look like a cruel and violent usurper, it gave justification for his overthrow by Elizabeth's ancestor, Henry VII. For that reason, Shakespeare may have depicted Richard III as such a negative character in his famous play.

It can be argued that the fact that Shakespeare and others made Richard III look bad, to please a Tudor monarch, doesn't change the fact that he might have been motivated to kill the princes to become king. Richard III's ruthless nature was not, however, unusual for a ruler of his time. To maintain power as a ruler during the fifteenth century, it was necessary to have a strong will and be open to taking whatever action was necessary to protect the power base. Since most heads of state in fifteenth-century Europe were capable of committing murder in order to achieve power, it is not helpful in determining what happened to the princes to inquire whether Richard III had the right temperament for murder, but instead whether there are facts that tend to show he was instrumental in the murder of his nephews.

Traditionally, it has been pointed out that Richard III

was in an ideal position to get rid of his nephews after he became king. Richard's station alone does not prove he liquidated his nephews. Why after Richard became king would he leave himself open to criticism and the vulnerability of revolution by killing his nephews? King Richard III may have still feared the ability of the Queen's family and supporters to rally people in support of the princes. As long as the boys lived, they could act as a rallying point for those that did not support Richard's rule. If the princes were not killed during Richard III's rule, then why did he not produce them during the Battle of Bosworth Field to prove that the rumors that he had murdered them were false?

There were other aspirants to the throne besides Richard of Gloucester after King Edward IV died. Discrediting the descendants of Edward IV left the throne open to not only Richard, but to other contenders such as the man who later became Henry VII and the Duke of Buckingham, who was at the time the constable of England. There is always the possibility that the declaration of the princes' illegitimacy came about not so much out of the direct actions of Richard, but through the influence of other people who wanted the downfall of the Queen and her children. Couldn't the man who later defeated Richard and became King Henry VII have been the real murderer of the children?

When Henry VII became ruler of England he had a contract to marry the princes' sister to further support his claim to the throne. It would do no good for the new king to marry the princes' sister if she was illegitimate. Henry VII made it a point after taking control of the government to make sure that all rumors that the children of Edward

IV were illegitimate were silenced and openly proclaimed his wife to be legitimate. By doing this, he automatically recognized the princes as legitimate and left himself open to challenges by them to having a prior claim if they still were alive. If the princes were alive in 1485, they would have been a real threat to Henry, so the best way to have secured his rule would have been to make sure that the princes were killed and to marry their sister at the earliest practical time. Henry VII did not initially, after taking the throne, accuse his predecessor, Richard III, of murdering the princes. If the princes survived their uncle's death, then that would explain why Henry VII did not at first make accusations against his predecessor that would have further supported and legitimized his actions in seizing the throne. Could the delay in accusing Richard have been because the princes were still alive at the time that Henry became king?

Accusations against Richard III and Henry VII may have been simply because they both were so much in the public eye. The real murderer could have been none other than Henry Stafford, who was the Duke of Buckingham. During the protectorate of Richard, the Duke of Buckingham was the Constable of England and had a claim of his own to the throne of England. As a holder of the title of Constable of England, he had access to the princes' royal apartments in the Tower of London. He could take advantage of his power by allowing access to people retained by him to murder the children. Once the royal youngsters were out of the way, he could blame their death on Richard III. This would leave him as an open candidate to succeed to the throne.

In support of Sir Thomas More and Shakespeare, who

accused Richard III of engineering the death of his nephews, is the fact that three centuries after the boys' alleged murders, two children's bodies were found under the stairway in the Tower of London. Unfortunately, a study conducted in the 1930s of the remains earlier found in the tower revealed that two complete skeletal remains were no longer in existence. It was not even possible to firmly substantiate that the skeletal remains available for study were from boys. A reconstruction of the bones seemed to indicate, however, that the skeletal structures were those of two children approximately the same age as the princes would have been when last publicly observed. It was not possible, however, to test for the exact date that the children had died. If the bones could be tested in such a way as to indicate the exact year the children had died, it might give a better indication of who really plotted their murder. If they were killed in 1483 during Richard's reign, he would be the most likely culprit. In the event their murder could be proven to be after 1485, then Henry VII may have been responsible for the princes' deaths. Unfortunately, the skeletal remains cannot be tested to pinpoint the exact year of death. The question of what happened to the lost English princes remains as debatable now as when Shakespeare's play Richard III was first performed during the reign of a Tudor monarch.

4

The True Identity of Prisoner Number 7— Rudolf Hess

When inmate Number Seven of Spandau prison died in 1987, the world took notice. It was not just because he was the last Nazi prisoner left from World War II, but because number seven claimed to be none other than Rudolf Hess the former deputy fuehrer of Germany. His death did not end the controversy and many questions surrounding him. For over forty years, he had been a living symbol of the leaders who had brought on the Holocaust and the terrible tragedies related to World War II. What type of man would participate in the creation of a fascist state that would disregard the basic rights of people? Was prisoner number seven really Rudolf Hess or an imposter? The answer to many of the questions about prisoner number seven, who claimed to be Rudolf Hess, may be found in what is known about the real deputy fuehrer of Germany.

Rudolf Hess was born in Egypt in 1894. His father was a successful German businessman. Rudolf's early years were spent attending a local school in Egypt that was taught along German lines. When the Hess family moved back to Germany in his later teenage years, his education continued in that country. When World War I broke out he enlisted in an infantry regiment. While serving in the army he was wounded three times. After hospitalization he joined the flying corps and completed his training as a pilot. In December of 1918, he left the military forces with a great deal of experience in war and wounds to show his service.

After the war he continued to experience, as a result of his wounds, shortness of breath and periodic attacks of bronchitis. Being in the army did not mean that Rudolf Hess gave up his propensity to violence. He participated in brawls and riots as a part of a burgeoning group that was known as the Nazis. A leader in the organization, Adolf Hitler, found young Hess to be an enthusiastic follower with not only a propensity for violence, but the intelligence to assist in forming strategies that would build the party. Rudolf Hess demonstrated an ability to organize and administer a group of agitators. Some have even credited him with being one of the major builders of the Nazi party that eventually took over control of Germany in the 1930s. In 1933, Hitler became chancellor of Germany and appointed Rudolf Hess as his deputy. This gave Hess an opportunity to influence a myriad of different institutions in German society.

By September of 1940, Hess appeared to believe that

Germany should center its attention on its real enemy to the East, which was Soviet Russia. It did not appear that he wanted to take Great Britain on as an enemy. Some Nazi leaders believed at the time that the English shared a common heritage with the Germans so they should not be at war with one another. An acquaintance of Hess encouraged him to try to make contact with the Duke of Hamilton, possibly for the purpose of developing a peace plan between Great Britain and Germany. There were efforts by other contacts to set up a meeting between the two countries in a neutral location.

In May of 1941, authorities in Great Britain made the surprising announcement to the world, that a man claiming to be Rudolf Hess had landed his plane in Scotland for the purpose of meeting with the Duke of Hamilton. Was the man, who landed in Scotland, telling the truth when he claimed to be Rudolf Hess? Why would Rudolf Hess have to travel all the way to Scotland to meet the Duke of Hamilton when he could have made contact with him through a neutral intermediary? Why would Rudolf Hess have taken the chance of flying to a hostile country, when he faced the possibility of arrest upon arrival at his destination? If Rudolf Hess voluntarily went without the permission of the Fuehrer on a secret peace mission from Germany to England, couldn't his actions have been interpreted by the Nazis as a sign of disloyalty?

There is evidence that Rudolf Hess drove his car to an airfield at Augsburg on May 10, 1941. There he donned a flight uniform and climbed into a Messerschmitt plane. Interestingly enough, the plane that was supposedly chosen had a range of approximately 850 miles under the best of conditions. Picking such a plane would be risky

Rudolf Hess

because Augsburg was about 850 miles away from his destination. In order to follow such a route, Hess would have to fly the plane in a path through a part of England that was well-guarded. There would be a chance that he would be shot down in the process. Wouldn't a skilled pilot like Rudolf Hess have chosen a plane that was equipped with long range fuel tanks, so that he could take a detour around the well-protected areas, to get to the Duke of Hamilton in Scotland? Did the real Hess flight reach Scotland or was it earlier intercepted by the Germans who substituted another pilot and plane for the journey? What was the actual flight plan of the pilot who landed in Scotland and claimed to be Hess? Was the plane that carried the alleged deputy fuehrer specially prepared for the flight?

There has never been a clear explanation why Hess chose to meet with the Duke of Hamilton. Although it is known that the Duke was well accepted by certain members of society in Great Britain, he was not one of the official leaders who could dramatically influence British policy. Could it be that the Duke of Hamilton was a part of a clandestine group of people who took exception to the foreign policy set by the key leaders in power in Great Britain? When the pilot parachuted into Scotland on May 10, 1941, his captors seemed to accept that the German prisoner was Rudolf Hess as he said he was at the time. If the man who parachuted into Scotland was really the deputy fuehrer of Germany, then why did he not possess any identification papers proving he was Rudolf Hess? It seemed that authorities found very little on the person of their captive that could support his story. A search revealed photographs and an envelope postmarked from

Munich which were very vague indicators that they had a German captive, but not of that person's exact identity.

It has been claimed that the captive had a camera that was later identified to have belonged to the wife of Rudolf Hess. Couldn't any German pilot have flown to Great Britain and claimed to have been Rudolf Hess? Is the possession of a camera that may have been owned by Rudolf Hess's wife enough to substantiate the pilot's story? Even the pilot's flying suit lacked any clear marking that would indicate its ownership. It is possible from available research that the real Rudolf Hess may have started out in a plane to fly over the North Sea, but vanished into oblivion. The man who bailed out in Scotland may very well have been his double, who set out from a destination in Norway. This could explain why the person who claimed to be the deputy fuehrer of Germany had no identification papers to substantiate his claim. What happened in the air flight of the real Rudolf Hess? Why would someone else have been substituted for him in the flight to Scotland?

Despite the fact that British authorities, who questioned the man claiming to be Rudolf Hess, accepted his identity there appear to be some discrepancies between what is known about the real Rudolf Hess and the man claiming to be him. The pilot who landed in Scotland supposedly had a healthy appetite, while the real Rudolf Hess was known to be quite a fussy vegetarian. The deputy fuehrer of Germany took pride in his appearance and had the bearing and manners of a gentleman, while the pilot had a tendency towards sloppiness and even a lack of interest in following traditional grooming practices. Rudolf Hess was known to take pride in his strong mental state and physical fitness, while the prisoner seemed to be excessively thin and required a great deal of attention from professionals such as psychiatrists.

Possibly even more confusing were the physical differences between the pilot who claimed to be Rudolf Hess and the deputy fuehrer of Germany. The real Rudolf Hess was known to have a gap between his teeth, while the claimant had no such gap. As a result of acting as a soldier during the war, Hess had received a lung wound which created problems at times with his breathing. The prisoner of war, later known by the code name of Jonathan, was a powerful walker who exhibited no difficulties at all with his breathing under hard physical exertion. A physical examination of the claimant revealed that he lacked the scars from the wounds that were known to have been on the body of Rudolf Hess. How could the captive be the former deputy fuehrer of the Third Reich when he did not exhibit the physical difficulties or scars known to be possessed by Rudolf Hess?

There has been a great deal of speculation as to the identity of the prisoner of war claiming to be Rudolf Hess. In addition, there still remain a number of other questions, including how and why a double was substituted for Hess? The theory has developed that Himmler, who was the head of the SS, may have learned that Rudolf Hess was going to travel to Scotland to meet with leaders there to try to develop a peace bridge between the two nations. As deputy fuehrer, Rudolf Hess stood in the way of Himmler gaining more power in Germany. Himmler developed a plot to eliminate the real Hess, in an effort to destroy his competition in the Nazi hierarchy. A double was enlisted who looked like Hess. The double was then trained with enough knowledge to play the part. When Hess passed over the North Sea his plane was shot down, while a second plane containing the imposter traveled to Great Britain. Possibly, it was the idea of Himmler that the actor playing the part of Hess could try to fulfill the real deputy fuehrer's goal. If he was successful in enlisting support for peace between the two nations then Himmler would take over the negotiations and establish credit for the overall success. In the event that Hess was captured as a prisoner or was unsuccessful in his mission, then he could be labeled a traitor, which would eliminate him as an obstacle to Himmler's reach for power.

It is known that Himmler aspired to take the top seat of power in Germany. He has been credited with plots even to overthrow Adolf Hitler. It would be consistent with his personality and previous conspiratorial actions to believe that he would take advantage of any opportunity to eliminate a rival, such as Rudolf Hess, who stood in the way of his movement for the absolute control of Germany.

Although Himmler's motivation for a substitute makes sense, it is not clear why a double for Rudolf Hess would not reveal his true identity after being captured in Scotland. Even if the prisoner did not originally admit the falsehood of his identity during World War II, why would he continue in his false role after the war ended? It has been theorized that the person playing Hess did not reveal his true identity out of fear for what might happen to his real family. It is known that the Nazis were capable of tremendous cruelty toward traitors. A double that was enlisted to play Rudolf Hess might fear that if he revealed the wrong information he would be signing the death sentence for any of his family who were left in Germany. Even after Himmler's demise, some people believe he still had supporters who were strong enough to take action against a traitor.

Despite the interesting theory of a double for Hess, the prisoner of war claiming to be him never made a slip in his words that would clearly show that he was not the former deputy fuehrer. Some people have argued that the lack of clear proof that the prisoner was an imposter was not because of his skill at impersonation, but rather because he was not openly interrogated by experts. The claimant was, however, questioned by intelligent and skilled interrogators. The interviews may not have been effective in determining the truth, since the prisoner claimed amnesia as an excuse for his lack of memory. As a result of the lack of substantial information provided by the prisoner, researchers have to piece together who he was from other sources. People who accept that the prisoner was, in fact, who he claimed to be, point out that Rudolf Hess's wife alleged that the handwriting of the prisoner of war was the same as her husband's. Despite the fact prisoner Number Seven in Spandau claimed to be Rudolf Hess, he resisted meeting with his wife and son in person for approximately twenty-eight years. The recurring excuse of amnesia was used whenever he was seriously questioned about his past. When Rudolf Hess's wife did have an opportunity to meet with the prisoner of war, she observed that his voice had changed so that it seemed much deeper now than it had in the past. Skeptics of the prisoner's claim to being Rudolf Hess have pointed out, that it seems unusual that his voice got deeper as he moved into old age.

It might have been expected that the passing of time would lessen the public's interest in the man who claimed to be Rudolf Hess. During the prisoner's long stay in Spandau the public's interest in him, however, never substantially waned. When inmate Number Seven in Spandau prison finally died on August 17, 1987, it only served to intensify interest in him. An intriguing additional question arose out of the fact that the man claiming to be Rudolf Hess was found in the garden pavilion of Spandau prison with a cord around his neck, which apparently had been used to strangle him to death. Investigations failed to establish whether the prisoner had died by suicide or assassination. Was the prisoner killed to eliminate the possibility that he would reveal the secrets that he had carried for so many years in his mind?

There were people who knew the prisoner of war who said he had expressed a genuine fear of lapsing into senility. Was Hess concerned that his emotional strength might weaken with age and that he would slip to reveal a bit of information that could endanger his family? Could the prisoner simply have engineered his own death by suicide to avoid the weaknesses brought on by age?

An argument has been made that given the prisoner's health at the time of his death he was incapable of physically setting up the length of cord in such a way as to cause his suffocation. It seems that even in death the questions surrounding the man who claimed to be Rudolf Hess have not been laid to rest. Unless some great revelations show up in clearly documented form from the Third Reich in Germany, the true identity of the pilot claiming to be Rudolf Hess and the cause of that person's death may never be resolved with a clear answer. The questions surrounding the deputy fuehrer of Germany may remain one of the great unanswered questions that came out of the terrible reign of terror unleashed by the Nazis against the world community.

5

The Man in the Iron Mask

The novel *The Man in the Iron Mask*, by Alexandre Dumas, has captured the interest of thousands of readers since its creation in the nineteenth century. The story may not, however, be totally fictitious, but the author's version of an actual unsolved historical mystery. Rumors of a man who was forced to live in prison behind a mask date back well over a century before the publication of Dumas's classic story. In 1703 it was rumored that a prisoner who was forced to live in a mask died in the Bastille in France. Supposedly, even his immediate jailers did not know his actual identity. Rumor had it that he was buried the next day under the name of Marchioly. In the middle of the eighteenth century the famous philosopher, Voltaire, immortalized the story of the man in the iron mask in relating the history of King Louis XIV. After Voltaire mentioned the story of the mysterious masked prisoner, theories abounded about the identity of the ancient prisoner and the reason for his unusual captivity.

Stories of the prisoner differ on the type of mask he was forced to wear. Even the tales that describe the mask as iron, differ on whether it was one solid mask or constructed out of separate metal parts that were connected. The latter type of metal mask may be described as having a large metal piece to cover the top half of the face with a hinge with springs attached on either side that were linked to a lower separate metal piece which covered the chin and could be drawn down to allow the prisoner to eat without removing the mask. Some versions of the story had the mysterious prisoner simply wearing a cloth or velvet mask that could easily be removed.

In the years that preceded Voltaire's revelation of the man in the iron mask the most generally accepted version of the story was that King Louis XIII had not been able to have a child by his wife, Ann of Austria. One of the leading advisors to the king had an affair with the queen. Out of that relationship Ann of Austria bore a son. Since the child was illegitimate, his birth was kept a secret. Later when the queen eventually gave birth to the man who later became known as the Sun King, Louis XIV, the queen's elder illegitimate child had to be put in prison behind a mask to conceal the obvious family resemblance. There always might be those people that would believe that the older child should have a prior claim to the throne even if he was illegitimate. By imprisoning him secretly with the requirement that he wear a mask, there would be very little chance that people would find out his actual identity and that France would

Alexandre Dumas, author of The Man in the Iron Mask

run the risk of civil war over his succession to the throne. Although this theory of Louis XIV's elder brother swayed some people, there were doubters who believed it did not seem entirely reasonable. Why would the queen's oldest son be a threat if it was not the practice for illegitimate children to succeed to the throne? Critics reasoned that just because a child was born of the queen it did not mean that he would necessarily look so similar to the ruling family that he would present a threat to the throne.

Possibly it was the controversy surrounding the mysterious prisoner that led to the theory that prevailed after Alexandre Dumas's book, *The Man in the Iron Mask*, was published. Many readers of Dumas's famous novel accepted the idea that the man in the iron mask was none other than a twin brother of Louis XIV. This was not a new theory, but had become prevalent by the end of the eighteenth century. Supposedly, Louis XIV was born far earlier in the day than his twin brother. The younger boy was then hidden to avoid civil war and problems with Louis XIV succeeding to the throne. Yet, even though the version of the twin brother of Louis XIV has been repeatedly told, it has never been substantiated.

Could the man in the iron mask have been the Duke of Monmouth, who was the illegitimate son of Charles II of England? Was the mysterious prisoner kept in France behind bars to avoid problems with the English succession? The theory that the man behind the mask was the son of Charles II is interesting, but lacks factual substantiation.

Some researchers have indicated that it was reasonable to believe that the mysterious prisoner was none other than an Italian by the name of Mattioli, who was a minister of the Duke of Mantua. The minister had been imprisoned because he had double-crossed Louis XIV who had been involved in some intrigue over border lands that had caused some political problems for the French king. The historical background of this minister is not entirely clear. He allegedly was known by the name of Ercole Mattioli, born in 1640, and served as the secretary of the Duke of Mantua. The minister has been accused of being guilty of some double dealing between France and another nation. The problem started when Louis XIV tried to acquire a part of a piece of neighboring Italian land which belonged to the Duke of Mantua. Secret negotiations took place to avoid public uproar and possible embarrassment to the Duke. He had a number of friends in Spain, who were quarreling with the King of France. The double dealing minister, Ercole Mattioli, supposedly leaked the news of Louis's negotiations to his Spanish enemies, which caused the deal to fall through.

The claim is that Louis XIV in his fury decided on a plan to punish the loose-mouthed minister. He lured him into French territory where he was arrested and thrown into prison. Another version of the story is that Louis paid Mattioli for the property, but the money was not turned over to his employer. The Italian duke refused to transfer the property, since he had not received the funds. In retaliation for Mattioli's dishonesty, Louis secretly sent several of his men to kidnap the minister and bring him to France where he was placed in prison. Both versions of the story explain, that to avoid public uproar, Louis made it look as though Mattioli had simply disappeared by making him wear a mask and putting him into a tightly guarded prison. It is said that one of the lieutenants of the Bastille had earlier referred to the masked person as M. Marchiel and that the prisoner was buried under the different name of Marchioly. The name Mattioli, is quite similar to both the name Marchiel that was mentioned as the prisoner's name by a lieutenant of the Bastille and the other name of Marchioly under which the prisoner was supposedly buried.

Does the similarity in the various names indicate that they all refer to the same prisoner? It has been reasoned that Mattioli was the true identity of the man and that the king kept his identity secret by making changes in his name so that it would not be easily recognized. Possibly the difference in the name may have been caused simply by different pronunciations of it, that when recorded and then recopied took on the form and sound of a different name. If Mattioli was a foreign minister, then why would he have to wear a mask to hide his identity from the prison guards? It would seem to be an unnecessary act to force a foreign prisoner to wear a mask when the people who would view him would not be familiar with his looks. Even if people did recognize him, it is not likely that they would have made contact with his countrymen nor that his homeland would go to war just simply because the former minister was in prison.

The French Revolution brought about the fall of the famous prison known as the Bastille. After the Revolution, the archives that were examined revealed some interesting facts about the elusive history of the prisoner. Nothing showed up in the records that indicated that Ann of Austria gave birth to an illegitimate son or twins.

The records did, however, reveal that there were stories circulating that Ann of Austria had an illegitimate son by the English Duke of Buckingham. The alleged affair was not, however, substantiated by factual data. The rumor was that the illegitimate male child was born in 1626. He supposedly bore a tremendous resemblance to the son born later to the queen, who was known as Louis XIV. Was the version of the illegitimate child born of a relationship with an English Duke nothing more than a red herring to throw people off the track of the prisoner's real identity?

The French archives mention an interesting individual of French extraction who could be a possible candidate for the identity of the man behind the mask. It seems that the Bastille records show that the man behind the mask was originally imprisoned in Pignerol, on the island of St. Margarite, as was the prisoner Mattioli. The records, however, indicate that Mattioli may have remained at Pignerol, while the man in the iron mask was moved along to a new location when the prison governor Saint-Mars moved to a different institution. Communications were found between Saint-Mars and the minister of war regarding the unusual prisoner. There were even letters that indicate the king was aware of the unusual arrangements that were made as to this special prisoner. The man behind the mask, according to these communications was Eustache Dougher, who was not allowed to give any information about himself or to send letters outside. Even the prison governor was warned to avoid listening to explanations that may be given by the special inmate. Apparently, Eustache Dougher possessed some terrible secret that even the king feared might be revealed. If Dougher knew too much, why was he imprisoned instead of executed? Could Dougher have had a special relationship with the royal family that kept him from being murdered or did Dougher hold onto some unknown secret that it was hoped might eventually be revealed to the king?

It seems that the prisoner Dougher has been referred to by some people as a valet. Legend has it that he was allowed to become the valet of Nicholas Fouquat when the former finance minister was imprisoned for taking public monies. If Dougher was kept apart from other prisoners, then why was Fouquat allowed to have extensive contact with him? Could it be that Fouquat already knew the secret of the man in the iron mask or was it simply because it was known that Fouquat would never be allowed to leave the prison?

In order to be able to shed light on the real identity of the man behind the mask, it is necessary to try and find out more about the background of Eustache Dougher and what he could have done that would have caused him to be placed in such unusual confinement. Research into birth records shows that there were various people born around the time the prisoner would have been born with similar names. The strongest candidate for the identity of the man behind the mask was an Eustache Oger, also referred to as Dougher, who was the son of an officer of Cardinal Richleau's musketeers. It seems that Eustache was something of a black sheep in the family. In his childhood he had, however, been a playmate for the young boy who was to be known later as King Louis XIV of France. Could it be that King Louis XIV did not execute Dougher because he was a childhood friend or did

Dougher have an important contact at court who influenced the king to show leniency towards him?

There was a huge governmental scandal during the reign of Louis XIV, regarding the participation of prominent people in clandestine unorthodox religious practices, which were considered to be dangerous to French morality. It has been rumored that wealthy women confessed to poisoning their husbands as a result of attending sacrilegious rituals at secret meetings. When the perpetrators of the mystic practices were caught, their careers and reputations were destroyed. Eustache Dougher may have been guilty of participating in these unorthodox black magic practices. If Dougher was one of the people who had been active in the secret rituals, then why would it be necessary to force him to wear a mask and be placed in such unusual imprisonment?

Some people have argued that Dougher may have shared with Fouquat the secret of a treasure that the King of France was seeking to find. Was the prisoner kept alive in the hope that he would some day reveal the exact location of the treasure to the King? Could it be that the King kept Dougher from talking to others to prevent their finding out about the location of the treasure?

It has been speculated that Dougher's imprisonment may have been related to a secret order called the Priory of Zion, that had the goal of putting into power a king from the former Merovingian Dynasty in France. Did Louis fear being deposed by one of the Merovingian descendants?

It has been argued that one of Louis XIII's ministers arranged for François Dougher to have fathered a child out of a relationship with the queen, Ann of Austria.

Louis XIV was the son born out of that relationship. He was to be the heir who would protect against the succession of a Merovingian king. This would make Eustache Dougher the half brother of King Louis XIV. Could it be that Eustache Dougher had a loose tongue, which made Louis XIV fear his publicly revealing that he was the king's half-brother or did Dougher actively try to blackmail the French king about his hidden secret? If Dougher was truly a half-brother who could not be trusted to keep the secret, it would explain why he was kept incognito and made to wear a mask. In this way, he could not tell of his relationship to the king and have his resemblance to Louis observed, which would substantiate the story.

Eustache Dougher may even have actively been involved in a plot to restore a Merovingian king to the throne of France. Could it be that Eustache was allowed to act as Fouquat's valet because both of them were aware of the secret that Louis XIV was not really the son of the former King Louis XIII, but instead the offspring of the same father as Eustache Dougher? The story that the queen of France had a baby by a substitute for the king seems similar to the rumor of a child born to the queen from a relationship with the Duke of Buckingham. Was the story of Ann of Austria's relationship with the Duke of Buckingham a purposeful diversion from the real fact that a substitute was used to create a royal heir or simply a confused version of the truth?

There is a story that when King Louis XV was told the secret of the man behind the mask, he claimed that if the prisoner was still alive he would set him free. If King Louis XV knew that the legitimacy of his ancestors was in question, would he be so willing to set the prisoner free or was King Louis XV so secure in his throne that he felt that such a secret no longer presented a threat? Louis XV has also been credited with explaining that if the truth was revealed it would show that the masked man's identity was not worth all the effort that had been made to find it. If the secret of the man behind the mask was not significant, why was he forced to stay behind a mask and held in a special prison cell incognito from other people? If Louis XV felt that the secret of the mysterious inmate was so unimportant, why did he not reveal the answer to the identity of the man behind the mask and the reason for his imprisonment? Speculation continues on the mysterious prisoner, who was made to wear a mask. The theories that come out of the speculation will no doubt continue to provoke argument on the fascinating period of time when Louis XIV ruled France.

6

Was There a Robin Hood?

Robin Hood has for centuries characterized the admirable qualities of a hero in western culture. The legend of the English bowman who robbed the rich to give to the poor has spread throughout the world. In the stories of Robin's exploits he has tremendous adventurous spirit, skill and leadership, which enable him to overcome obstacles successfully with the help of his companions. For several centuries, Robin Hood has served as a hero of the people. Modern heroes like Batman and Superman may have been based on the legendary bowman of Sherwood forest. Was Robin Hood a fictional character like Superman, or a real hero?

There is no general agreement among scholars, as to the origin of the Robin Hood character. Some people believe that Robin Hood is merely a product of ancient mythology. They point out that he may have developed out of the stories of ancient pagan gods who were celebrated at various festivals. It is reasoned that Robin's clothing is similar to a spirit of the woods since in ancient times wood spirits were said to have worn green. Could Robin Hood have been one of the characters celebrated during ancient May Day ceremonies who evolved over time into a mythical hero?

Despite the reasonableness of the connection of Robin Hood with ancient ceremonial characters, there appears to be possible evidence that the English hero of Sherwood Forest may actually have lived in the past. There is disagreement on Robin Hood's background, even among people who believe that he was a real person. Various periods of history have been alleged as the time when he lived.

Some people have argued that he was a character who lived at the same time as King Arthur. This would place him approximately in the sixth century A.D. It is significant to note, however, that there is not even universal acceptance of the existence of King Arthur, let alone any substantiating facts to show that a Robin Hood hero existed during the famous ruler's time. Have King Arthur and Robin Hood been placed in the same era because they both supposedly shared an interest in protecting the rights of the common people? Despite their common popularity, the British heroes were really quite different from one another. King Arthur stood for the proposition that might is not right, and that might should be used for right. In other words, King Arthur was a hero who believed that the law was the great regulator and protector of human beings. Robin Hood, on the other hand, would not have been a person who necessarily agreed with the idea that the law was the primary protector of people. After all, Robin Hood was known to take the law into his own hands and to operate in his own way no matter what the law said.

If King Arthur was the great law giver, then Robin Hood was the liberator of the common people from the injustices brought about by laws that were either unfair or unevenly enforced. It is inconsistent to believe that King Arthur and Robin Hood would have been fighting for the same goals, or even for that matter have lived at the same time period. If King Arthur actually lived, it would have been in the early Dark Ages when there was need for a leader to keep order through respect for the law. Robin Hood was more likely to have been a product of the end of the Middle Ages, when the peasant class started to break away from the social shackles that held them to the land.

Some tales connect Robin Hood with King Richard the Lionhearted. Once again there is a coupling effect between two great English heroes. It does not, however, seem likely that Robin Hood would have operated freely in Sherwood Forest during the reign of Richard the Lionhearted, which was around the end of the twelfth century, since legends of him did not really begin to become popular until at least a couple of centuries later.

Probably the biggest boost to the pairing of Robin Hood with King Richard the Lionhearted came out of Sir Walter Scott's classic book *Ivanhoe*, published in the nineteenth century. *Ivanhoe* served as the prototype for many of the tales, plays, and even movies that followed on the adventures of Robin Hood.

A lithograph depicting Robin Hood

There are many people who believe that Robin Hood was actually a nobleman, Sir Robin of Locksley, or the Earl of Huntington, who left the luxuries of his noble birth to live in the forest and fight the injustices perpetrated upon the common people. If Robin Hood was a noble, would he be anxious to break down the privileges of his class? Although the romantic tale of a noble Robin Hood has become well accepted, it appears to be inconsistent with the earlier tales and ballads of the bandit of Sherwood Forest. It seems that in the late Middle Ages Robin Hood was described as a yeoman. Would it make better sense for a free man, who owned his own land, or a noble to become a hero to the common people? As a yeoman he could act as a representative of the people since he understood what it would be like to be a small tenant farmer, who was barely above that of the landlord's peasants. The ballads of Robin Hood seem to signal a call to arms to break the chains of the oppressed peasant class held by the nobles.

One of the persistent problems in trying to track down the original Robin Hood is that over time there was more than one person with a similar name who could have acted as a source for the legendary hero. It is not clear whether Robin Hood was a complete creation of fiction, a mythical character based on a composite of several real people, with possibly similar names or one actual person whose exploits served as a model for the legendary hero. Were fictional elements added over time to the actual adventures of a real hero to create the legendary Robin Hood?

In the middle of the nineteenth century a review of historical documents in England revealed information about a person who could have been the original Robin Hood. It seems that there actually was a person by the name of Robert Hood. He was born around 1290 and lived in Wakefield, Yorkshire, England. During that period of time people with the name of Robert were often given the nickname of Robin. In the beginning of 1316, Robert Hood and his wife paid for the right to a small piece of ground.

This was during the reign of the rather unpopular King Edward II. His lack of attention to proper administration of matters of state lead to tremendous public discontent and a desire to remove him from the English throne. Records from the time, indicate that Robert Hood may have joined the army of the Earl of Lancaster, to fight against the unpopular king. The Lancaster army was defeated and his supporters were declared outlaws. One of the pieces of property that was confiscated is in the immediate area of Robert Hood's land. He may have been forced, after the unsuccessful revolt by Lancaster and the taking of his land, into the forest. Robert Hood along with other refugees may have lived off the deer population in the forest.

At the time, approximately one-third of the land of England was owned by the king. The forest around Yorkshire and Nottingham would have been under his ownership. To kill royal deer was a serious crime that would have called for the exacting of terrible penalties upon the perpetrators. No doubt, those people who were willing to brave the risk of such penalties and had not given up to the unpopular rule of King Edward II would seem like heroes.

If Hood became a folk hero he may have been referred

to by the popular nickname of Robin. Possibly, the Robin Hood legends were told as a vehicle to encourage the peasants to break free of the bonds of an unpopular king and the nobles who supported him. Robin Hood may not, however, have remained in the forest as an outlaw for very long.

There may have been some truth to the legend that the hero of the forest actually had a confrontation with the king. It seems that Edward II was known to have been hunting in the spring of 1323 in the area of Wakefield. He was, however, surprised to find less deer than he was accustomed to hunting. Instead of hordes of deer to hunt he had a hard time finding even an individual specimen to shoot at. As a result, he supposedly blamed Robin Hood and his outlaw band for the terrible decimation of the creatures that had provided the pleasurable pastime of hunting.

Ballads relate that the king disguised himself as an abbot leading a group of his men dressed as monks to confuse the bandits of Sherwood Forest, and to lure Robin Hood into a trap. According to legend the king's ruse was effective enough to draw Robin Hood and his men out of hiding. The outcome was not, however, as expected. The king was so impressed with the bandits cordiality that an offer was made for Robin Hood to join the royal household as a valet. Records of a monthly payment to a Robyn Hod have supposedly been found, which would indicate that the bandit took the king's offer of employment. The records of payment show that Robyn stayed for a very short time in the king's employment. After about a year, could the royal employee have yearned to once again roam the forest? The exact reason why he left the king's employment is speculative. If Robyn really was the legendary hero of Sherwood Forest, he may have yearned to once again roam the forest, or been dissatisfied with his new position.

The man known as Robyn Hod, or Robin Hood, apparently continued to live as a bandit until around 1346, when he died. Why was Robin Hood able to successfully continue as a bandit for so many years after leaving the royal court? Did he survive because the force of his personality won the king's favor or was he truly a master of deception such as chronicled in the legend? After Robin Hood left the court, the king may have been so absorbed in domestic problems that he did not have time to center his attention on putting a stop to the bandit's criminal career. It is also possible that the king's son, who later became Edward III, may have met the famous bandit when he had been in his father's employment and out of admiration refrained from pursuing a course to catch him.

It is possible, however, that the Robyn Hod who lived during King Edward II and King Edward III's reigns was not the person who served as the prototype for the legendary hero. There is a school of thought that believes that Robin Hood may have lived in the earlier time of approximately A.D. 1230, during the reign of King Henry III. Records allegedly indicate that the Sheriff of Yorkshire was in possession during that period of time of property of an outlaw, commonly known as Robyn Hode. One argument in favor of the earlier date for Robin Hood's existence would be that it would have given a greater amount of time to pass for the ballads and legend of Robin Hood's life to have developed into the significant force that was present by the end of the Middle Ages.

During the sixteenth century, a tale circulated that Robin Hood had earlier been buried in a tomb with a stone over it. There seems to be different descriptions of the appearance of the grave. One version has Robin Hood's gravestone specifically inscribed with information about the deceased bandit and another claimed that the stone simply had a cross on it. Unfortunately, even if the stone truly had existed, there is a possibility that it was broken up for use by the navy. In the early part of the nineteenth century the navy did that. To people who believe Robin Hood was buried in the grounds of a nunnery, the fact that the navy used old gravestones explains why Robin Hood's remains have not been located in the twentieth century.

The Robin Hood legend may have developed during the late Middle Ages, out of the growing resentment of the common people to being oppressed by the nobility. The peasants' revolt against the extreme power of the nobles was one of the signs that the Middle Ages was drawing to an end. Recognition of the people's right to freedom may have become an integral part of the legend of the heroic bandit of Sherwood Forest. Whether Robin Hood was a real person or simply a fictitious hero, he stands as a symbol for the belief that a sole individual can bring together the force of the people to right the wrongs of society.

7

The Czar's Empty Coffin

A mysterious stranger who had the rough appearance of a nomadic wanderer rode a white horse into a small Siberian village in the fall of 1836. He had a singular presence, that made him stand out to observers. A curious law enforcement officer approached the stranger at a nearby blacksmith's shop. The officer asked the newcomer to identify himself and explain why he was visiting their town. After failing to answer the policeman's questions, he was flogged and imprisoned as a vagrant.

When the Grand Duke Michael, who was the younger brother of Czar Alexander I of Russia, learned of the arrest he threatened to punish the authorities for what they had done. After talking with the prisoner, Michael reluctantly agreed not to follow through with his threats. The city officials released the prisoner and the Grand Duke left town. The stranger also moved on to other places. Who was the mysterious stranger that warranted a Grand Duke traveling to a small town in Siberia to act as his protector? Why wouldn't the stranger reveal his identity and purpose in visiting the town?

It was later rumored that the same enigmatic stranger finally settled down in 1842, in the small town of Krasnorechensk, to live the life of a pious hermit. He was known to the people in the area as Fyodor Kuzmitch. The recluse lived alone in a small hut in the woods where he worked and prayed. To those who observed him, he seemed to be a model of religious piety. It seemed unusual to some people, however, that Kuzmitch went to church regularly but refused to take communion. Even more interesting to the town people in his area, was that the lonely hermit kept up regular communications with famous people throughout Russian society. Why would a religious recluse get the attention of prominent people, including the Russian nobility? Why would a man who obviously was well known by so many Russian notables choose to live by himself in the forest? Did Kuzmitch have another secret identity that was hidden from the people of his town?

Rumors began to develop about the possible true identity of Fyodor Kuzmitch. Some people believed that he was the former Czar of Russia, Alexander I. Officially, Alexander had died in 1825. After the Czar's death, however, questions were raised over the ruler's last days that led some people to question whether the Russian monarch had really died in the way and on the date recorded by the government. Could the Czar have chosen to abdicate his throne by faking his death? Did

Alexander I pretend to die and then assume the role of a pious hermit?

In order to assess the possibility that the rumors were true, it is necessary to look back at what is known about the background of Alexander I. Czar Paul I, who was Alexander I's father, was known to be an autocratic ruler who was feared and hated for the way that he treated nobles and commoners alike. The official line that was given to the public was that Paul I died of apoplexy. The unofficial story that has been passed down for generations is that on March 23, 1801, a group of notable men proceeded up the back staircase to Paul's chambers. When a sentry tried to stop them he was immediately cut down. The emperor tried to avoid a confrontation by hiding. Unfortunately for him, he was unsuccessful. He was found concealed behind a screen by the fireplace. When one of the conspirators slapped him across the face, he pushed the assaulting person back. As a result, a struggle ensued and Paul ended up being kicked and finally strangled to death. His son, Alexander I, succeeded to the throne, but not with all of the family pride that would normally be expected when a son succeeds his father to the throne.

Alexander may have come into power under a cloud because he felt guilty as a result of the terrible way that his father's rule had ended. If the new Czar felt guilty about what happened to his father, he did not immediately take it out on his subjects. Instead, he set about a course to develop a more humane and socially responsible government. Public welfare programs were planned along with other reforms that would bring the living standard of the average person to a higher level. Alexander

Czar Alexander I of Russia

even reviewed the prospects of abolishing the system of serfdom existing in Russia at the time. Despite apparently sincere efforts, the social improvement plans of the Czar fell short of their goal. The Czar may have had tremendous power, but the programs could not be implemented without the cooperation of his country's nobility. Russian aristocracy was not yet ready at the beginning of the nineteenth century to lose their privileged place in society. As a result, the Russian nobles undermined the Czar's social efforts and worked to solidify their authoritarian control over everyday living.

If Alexander's social programs ended in a dismal failure, then at least his foreign relations program appeared to show some success. In July of 1807, the Czar was successful in working out an agreement with the terror of the continent, Napoleon Bonaparte. This treaty kept Russia, at least for a time, safe from the ravages of the French ruler's ambitious warfare. It also bought time for Alexander to prepare his country for the possibility of war, should Napoleon later change his mind and abrogate the treaty. When Napoleon decided to invade Russia in June of 1812, it was the beginning of the end of his glorious military success. In Russia he found an opponent who successfully managed to leave him in a position where his troops could not get adequate supplies to survive on. When the cold Russian winter set in Napoleon was forced to recognize the dangerous situation that he was in. Many of his troops suffered from starvation and the freezing cold. Eventually, even Napoleon's great spirit was deflated and he was forced to retreat back toward his own country. As Napoleon's star fell, so rose the prestige of Alexander I, who was successful for the first time in inflicting a humiliating setback on the Grand Army of France.

All of the major countries of Europe now looked at Alexander I as one of the great leaders in Europe. He did not, however, appear to revel in the glory that came out of the victory over the French. Although Alexander had never shown a tremendous interest in religion as a youngster, after the defeat of Napoleon he showed an increasing interest in studying the Bible and philosophic discussions with friends over important matters of morality. When Napoleon was no longer a military threat and had been sent into exile, Alexander presented a plan to the other major rulers of Europe to establish a covenant of a holy alliance. It was similar in some respects to the proposal that was sponsored after World War I to establish a League of Nations that was proposed by American president Woodrow Wilson. Even though the foreign representatives were skeptical of the concept of a holy alliance, Alexander's prestige was so high that they were reluctant to reject it outright. To many people it seemed that Alexander I was a symbol of success, because of the tremendous role that he played in both defeating Napoleon and attempting to secure peace in Europe. Alexander, however, seemed to show no great pleasure in the high respect and success he had achieved in war and foreign policy. He seemed to exhibit an increasing disillusionment with his ability to handle the responsibilities of the crown. The early failure of his regime to secure substantial reforms seemed to weigh terribly upon him.

By 1819, Alexander was already discussing the idea that his brother, Nicholas, should succeed him to the throne. He expressed a desire to have Europe led by young, strong monarchs who could exert an enthusiastic spirit of leadership. Alexander increasingly began to pull away from the responsibilities of his office. It seemed that in 1825, he reached a low point of enthusiasm for the responsibilities of his position as Czar. When his wife became ill that year, he suggested that they move to an obscure retreat away from the capitol to live a quiet life. The once large Russian court who served the Czar was reduced to a handful of servants and doctors.

Living in a small town away from the pressures of court seemed to agree with the royal couple, but at times Alexander still showed his disappointment with his past lack of accomplishment in domestic matters and desire to be free of the shackles of power for all time. In October of that year, Alexander went on an expedition to the Crimea, to review his military forces. There was speculation at the time that Alexander was really setting the stage for a plan to later invade the Ottoman Empire.

When Alexander returned home in the middle of November, he appeared to be pale, tired, and disheartened. As the days rolled on, he complained of headaches, nausea, and other physical discomfort. The doctors who attended him did not, however, agree on what was causing the Czar's illness. Some of the people that were around him thought that he had a case of malaria, while some others thought that the symptoms were more like typhus. It is interesting that there were not only discrepancies as to what type of illness the Czar was suffering from, but also how he felt on a particular day. For example, a doctor who was treating him noted that the Czar's condition was deteriorating, while at the same time his wife expressed that he was feeling better and in good spirits. Up until November 23, 1825, the Czarina, Elizabeth, kept a regular diary that included sections on the Czar's condition. For an unexplained reason, the descriptions of the Czar's condition seemed to be unavailable after that time. On December 1, 1825, Alexander I, Czar of all of Russia, was declared dead.

Contrary to the custom at the time, a priest was not present throughout the final days of the Czar's illness. No autopsy of the Czar's body took place until over a day and a half later. The doctor's final report was less than conclusive in ending questions about the illness that could have killed the Russian ruler. The doctor's description of the condition of the deceased's body was inconsistent with the previous medical condition of Alexander I. Equally puzzling was that the physician did not reach a clear conclusion as to the details of the medical condition that lead to the Czar's death. The situation became increasingly confusing when a doctor later denied signing the Czar's death certificate and claimed that his signature had been a forgery. Alexander's mother could not wait for the Czar's remains to be returned to the capital, but instead, met the funeral train en route to identify her son's body. Although the Russian ruler's mother later claimed that the body she viewed was her son's, the question remains why she had felt it was necessary to rush ahead to meet the funeral train to identify the dead body of the Czar.

Rumors began to spread soon after the Czar's death about the curious circumstances that surrounded the end of his reign. There were some people who questioned why medical reports of the people around the

Czar differed as to his condition on particular days. Did the Russian monarch orchestrate a plan with key people that surrounded him to fake his death? Was the Czarina a party to a conspiracy to create a false pattern of illness for the Czar that would support a later claim that he had died?

An interesting theory that came out of the questions that surrounded the Czar's death was that Alexander supposedly had substituted a dead courier's body for his own. There were other people who believed that the Czar's coffin contained no corpse at all, but was filled with rocks. Over the years, cycles of interest in the actual fate of Alexander I escalated and waned.

After the Russian Revolution rumors again grew, when revolutionary leaders began digging up graves of the Czars, and supposedly found that the coffin of Alexander I was empty. If Alexander I had not really died in 1825, then what became of the great reformer? Could Fyodor Kuzmitch have been the real Czar Alexander I?

If Alexander I abdicated the throne, then the answer to what happened to him afterwards may be found in tales about the recluse Fyodor Kuzmitch. Later in his life he supposedly acted as a protector for a young peasant girl. He saw to it that she was educated and exposed to important religious concepts. As a part of her continuing education, she was sent off on pilgrimages to key holy places in Russia. The hermit provided her with letters of introduction to notable Russians who could be of help in her travels. She later claimed to have noticed that Kuzmitch showed a remarkable physical resemblance to a large portrait of Alexander I that she observed at a nobleman's home. The hermit who had taught her and looked after her interests for so long, even placed his hands on his belt in the same way as portrayed in the image of Alexander I in the portrait. After returning to her home, she allegedly confronted Kuzmitch with the resemblance. There was no open denial by him. Instead he started to shed tears and left the room. She later married a military man and established a home in Kiev. After some time passed, she returned to the hermit's home and learned he had passed away.

Legend has it that the recluse left behind a small pouch that had been carried around his neck by a cord. A coded message was found inside the pouch that was supposedly written by Czar Paul I to his wife to inform her that their son had been a party to a conspiracy. The coded message seemed to substantiate the theory that Alexander I had carried the tremendous guilt of his father's death with him in mind and on paper daily.

Did the terrible weight of the circumstances surrounding Alexander's succession to the throne eventually lead him to abdicate his role as possibly the most powerful monarch in Europe? Did Alexander I really give up his power to live as a recluse, or was the story that Alexander lived as a hermit a myth created because he was so great a ruler that some people did not want to see his life end in an ordinary way? Alexander I managed to stir controversy both in life and death.

8

Was There a King Arthur?

A young man grabs the handle of a sword that is entrenched in a large stone. He tries to extract the weapon, to no avail. The decision is made to try once again. This time, he concentrates his mind and strength on the goal and the sword slips out of its imprisonment. By extracting the legendary sword Excalibur, the young man has won himself a kingdom. He becomes King Arthur of England, the legendary ruler who established the round table of knights and the principle that might is not right, but instead that might must be used for right. A strong commitment to social responsibility supposedly led him to found a system of law that would bind both noble and commoner alike. He has been depicted as a courageous, powerful, compassionate, and insightful leader. The story of Arthur has become so popular that admiring fans from Wales, Cornwall, Northern England, Scotland, and even

France all claim he was one of their ancient ancestors. There are some people, however, who doubt that King Arthur lived. Was King Arthur a mythical figure, or was he a real man whose contribution was so great to society that stories of him have been perpetuated over time?

Most stories of King Arthur seem to show him as a leader of a knightly order. Members of his famous round table are often depicted in heavy suits of armor showing their physical prowess at jousts. Tales of Camelot roughly resemble what we know English court life was like in the twelfth and thirteenth centuries. Was there an actual king in England during the late Middle Ages who was similar to Arthur?

After William the Conqueror seized England in 1066, there was excellent documentation of the kings who followed him. There does not appear to be a real king of England during the twelfth or thirteenth century who could have been the prototype for King Arthur. This does not mean, however, that there never was a King Arthur, but rather that a search for the legendary monarch must go further back in time than the period generally ascribed to the knights of the round table. If there was a King Arthur, he might not have had the gentle and majestically beautiful type of court life that would be expected in twelfth and thirteenth century England or France. Was King Arthur depicted in the late Middle Ages because legends of him became extremely popular during that period?

A search of history before the Norman invasion of 1066, shows that there may have been a leader by the name of Arthur back at the beginning of the sixth century. It is not clear, however, that Arthur was the king of

King Arthur (near the back) *and his Round Table*

all of England as in the legendary tale, but rather that he was a great general who led his countrymen to defend against the Germanic invaders.

The Romans had held England for approximately four hundred years. During that time, many of the Roman occupiers became assimilated with the native people in England. After the Goths sacked Rome in A.D. 410, Roman troops were withdrawn to protect their homeland. This is the beginning of what is known as the Dark Ages. England especially was affected by the Roman withdrawal because quarrels broke out between local leaders, each of whom claimed to be a king.

At the same time, there were waves of invaders from Europe who wanted to take over the wealth of the English countryside. Angles, Jutes, and Saxons came across the North Sea to overrun England. The Celtic kings had a difficult time defending against the powerful invaders. There was at this time a great general by the name of Arthurus, who may have served as the source for the legendary character of King Arthur. It is not clear just what role this general may have played in resisting the invading forces. Could Arthurus have led the combined forces of the Celtic kings in defending against the Saxon invaders? Could General Arthurus have become a king himself because of his success in defending England or was he first the king of a small area of Britain and later given the command of other kings' forces to provide a united front against the Saxon invaders? It is not clear whether Arthurus was the commanding general of the united forces of the Celtic kings or a powerful king who orchestrated the deployment of Celtic soldiers against the enemy.

Arthur, the great commander, may have been the offspring of a Patrician Roman father and a noble British mother. Children of noble birth, during the beginning of the Dark Ages in Britain, were often trained as field officers in their youth. The education was similar to what a Roman soldier would undergo to become a field officer. Intense training in horsemanship, hand to hand combat, the use of weapons and tactics was provided to the student. This special type of education may have helped Arthur to successfully resist the invading forces from Europe.

There are indications that Arthur may originally have been from the area of Great Britain near the Hadrian Wall, that has come to divide Scotland and England. He may have commanded the area near the Antonine and Hadrian Walls that had earlier been built by the Romans to protect against invading barbarians from the north. Arthur may even have taken over the command of fighting forces made up of people of Roman descent whose ancestors had earlier acted as legionnaires in the area.

To find the truth behind the Arthurian legend it may be useful to study the reference that was made by the early chronicler Nennius in approximately the year A.D. 811 to an Arthur, who fought against the invading Saxons in the days when there were kings of Britain. Nennius described various battles that were participated in by Arthur. The exact years and locations where the battles took place are not clear today. Various interpretations of the writings of Nennius have been made that show a range of time for the battles anywhere from the end of the fourth and fifth centuries to as late as approximately the year A.D. 518.

Probably the greatest single source that researchers have looked to to find the truth of the King Arthur legend are the writings of Geoffrey of Monmouth. In his history of the kings of Britain, he described King Arthur. His writings may have been later used by Sir Thomas Malory in the creation of his classic Le Morte d'Arthur, which in turn, spawned many of the popular tales about King Arthur and his court. Geoffrey's history of the kings of Britain depicts Arthur as far more than even a king. He is a great leader who pursued an almost holy mission to rescue his world from the chaos and dangers of terrible outside forces. Later readers have interpreted these writings of Geoffrey to mean that Arthur was a king. His exact role, however, has been disputed by others who claim that Arthur was not necessarily a king, but instead a great general, who commanded the united troops of other kings.

Geoffrey's critics have questioned where he found his facts. Dates related to Geoffrey of Monmouth's lifetime have not been fully agreed upon by historians. A tentative date when he may have lived was around 1136. It is believed that his history of Arthur was written at the beginning of the twelfth century. It is known that by the end of the twelfth century fictional tales and fables of Arthur began to abound. This may have been the result of the great popularity of Geoffrey's earlier work on the history of the kings of Britain that contained a great deal of information on King Arthur. Geoffrey may have taken some artistic license in describing the great leader Arthur. This does not, however, necessarily mean that Arthur did not live. It is not unusual for a writer hundreds of years after a period of time to exaggerate or even use information from other mythical sources to puff up a leader or make stories of him more interesting. Information gathered from a variety of different sources including Geoffrey of Monmouth, research by other historians, traditional Welsh stories of Arthur, and stories that circulated for years in Europe support the argument that there was an actual Arthur, who may have been the commander in chief of the Celtic forces that resisted the Saxons. He may have also been a king himself.

The available information tends to show that Arthur may have been born somewhere in the period of A.D. 475. In order to mount the great battles that were described by Geoffrey, Arthur would have been elected the commander in chief by the Northern forces in England somewhere in the period of A.D. 490 to A.D. 500. There may even have been a peaceful period after the great victory by Arthur. This temporary period of rest, may have acted as a source for the stories of the idyllic existence at King Arthur's court.

Unfortunately, there is not a single translation that is universally accepted of Geoffrey of Monmouth's original text. Translations differ, for example, on the exact location of King Arthur's home base. Arguments have been made for the location of Camelot anywhere from Cornwall to Scotland. It does not necessarily mean that Geoffrey of Monmouth was not accurate, but that his later readers have a difficult time translating what he said, especially on the subject of geography. The question also arises whether Geoffrey actually had the resources to find the exact geological locations of King Arthur's battles at the time he wrote his history. It appears that Arthur as a commanding general brought his troops to fight at various sites across Britain. There are indications that the great general may have made his home base somewhere in the area of England or Scotland. There is still no definitive proof, however, that the famed city of Camelot ever existed. Some researchers believe that the name may have been created by poets in the twelfth century in order to create the right atmosphere for the legendary king.

All researchers do not, however, agree that Camelot is a fictional place. Some historians have carefully studied the writings of Nennius and others who followed, in order to try to piece together information that would give landmarks that could be used to pinpoint the real location of Camelot. Unfortunately, the research as yet has not been able to prove just one location, but instead has been used to argue for various spots throughout Great Britain. A possible stronghold has been found, that may have been used at a time when Arthur could have lived, at South Cadbury Hill. The ancient hill fort that may have existed there is not, however, the only one that could have existed in Great Britain at the time Arthurus may have resisted the Saxons, nor is there conclusive evidence that the hill fort that may have existed at Cadbury actually was, in fact, the home of Arthur. One argument that has been put forward in favor of Cadbury Hill as Camelot is that it is very close in distance to Glastonbury Abbey where one legend says that King Arthur was buried.

The story has long been told that King Arthur and his wife's remains were discovered in the year A.D. 1190 in a hollow tree deep down in the ground near Glastonbury Abbey. Later the skeletal remains were exhumed and transferred to a tomb in the church. King Edward I allegedly opened that tomb in 1278, and found that the bones showed that King Arthur was a man, who appeared to be quite tall and powerful. The tomb was supposedly destroyed during the Reformation period.

The date and place where King Arthur passed away has been open to a great deal of speculation. The dates for King Arthur's death range anywhere from A.D. 515 to A.D. 542. Even the exact way that Arthur died has been argued over by historians. One version is that Arthur may have been fatally wounded at Camlon near the Hadrian Wall. Other versions say that King Arthur never died in England, but instead may have gone off to fight other wars on the continent as the last protector of the Roman civilized world in Northern Europe. Still other people prefer to accept the legend that he was wounded and then taken to the mystical island of Avalon to end his life.

A widely circulated romantic tale is that King Arthur sleeps in a huge cavern within Cadbury Hill. Supposedly, somewhere in the area of Cadbury Hill there is a large flat stone that provides access to King Arthur's final resting place. One man at the end of the nineteenth century even claimed to have found a stone in the area. When it was allegedly uncovered, it was discovered that it led to a cave. Unfortunately, the location of the stone was never recorded. Some people even assert that King Arthur awakens twice a year on Midsummer's Eve and Christmas Eve to ride again. This is based on stories that have been told of the sound of horses hoofbeats that have been heard in the area of Cadbury Hill.

Even though there is a great deal of conjecture about King Arthur, there is general acceptance that stories of him have had a tremendous impact on western civilization. He may have been killed off in various ways at different times in legends, but the stories themselves will live on for an eternity. These marvelous tales will survive because they describe the admirable qualities of leadership of the man who has come to be known as King Arthur of England.

9

Who Discovered America?

For many years, Columbus has been credited with the discovery of the New World in 1492. The story of how Queen Isabella of Spain sold her jewelry to pay for Columbus's trip has taken on legendary proportions. Was America discovered by the single milestone voyage of Columbus for Spain or has Columbus been credited with being the discoverer because he was the first visitor to America to permanently establish commerce and firm ties between the New World and the Old World?

The New World may have been visited in ancient times by visitors from the Northern part of Europe. Evidence to support this claim has shown up in Canada, where distinctive marks found in the ground may be an ancient calendar. It has been estimated that the marks were made in approximately 1700 B.C. There have been changes in climatic conditions over the centuries. It has been reasoned that over 3,500 years ago the northern waters were substantially warmer than they are today. Adventurous spirits from Northern Europe could have crossed the Atlantic ocean to develop commercial colonies in North America. Possibly, this may help explain the mystery of what appears to be ancient mines near the Great Lakes area. There is not firm evidentiary proof, as yet, to substantiate claims that visitors from Europe came to America as early as 1700 B.C. There are, however, some indications that at a far later time, pre-Columbian explorers from Scandinavian countries arrived in the New World.

Ancient legends tell that the Vikings explored far Western regions of land during the Middle Ages. Erik the Red, who was the father of Leif Ericson, supposedly went to explore the Western land beyond the sea. Leif Ericson, who was a skilled sailor, may have ventured even farther, after the year 1000, to the land that is now known as North America. A settlement was established in an area of land that the Vikings called Vinland. Whether this was the first settlement of Northern Europeans still remains a hotly debated issue. Researchers in modern times found evidence of what may have been a Viking colony at L'Anse aux Meadows in Newfoundland. Ancient foundations of houses and possibly cooking pits, have been found in the area. This could support the story of Leif Ericson's early travel to the New World.

Some scholars have suggested that the Newport tower, which is a small stone structure in Newport, Rhode Island, also supports the idea that the Vikings were in America before Columbus. Other historians have argued

Leif Ericson, who may have come to America before Columbus

that the building in Rhode Island was more likely built in the seventeenth century. Objects that have been found are often used to further bolster the theory that there in America were pre-Columbian Norsemen, who explored the New World.

One of the more hotly contested artifacts is the Kensington Rune Stone, which was discovered in Douglas County, Minnesota, in 1898. The runic characters on the stone, supposedly tell the story of Scandinavian travelers who were exploring America in 1362. Some researchers believe that the stone's carvings may be authentic, which would substantiate that the Vikings visited the New World before the time of Columbus. Other scholars believe that the stone is nothing but the creation of a jokester, or group of people for a hoax.

Another object that has been the subject of debate is the Vinland Map. It was supposedly drawn in the middle of the fifteenth century, approximately fifty years before Columbus sailed to America. The map allegedly depicts North America, which would substantiate that the New World was discovered far in advance of the exploration of Columbus. Not everyone has accepted the map as authentic. Detractors argue that an ink analysis has shown that the map may be the creation of a modern-day forger. Would a modern-day map drawer be able to accurately depict knowledge of the world through the eyes of a person in the Middle Ages? The verdict is not in on the authenticity of the map, and the arguments rage on over what role the Vikings may have played in the discovery of pre-Columbian America.

Scandinavian discoverers are not the only possible visitors to the New World before Columbus. Suggestions have been made that people from the British Isles may have visited the New World at a very early date in time. There is an area called Mystery Hill near North Salem, New Hampshire, where there is a clustered group of stone structures that appear to have been created by people. On these structures are carvings that have been interpreted as being the creation of people of Celtic origin. The writings are ancient enough that they have been estimated as dating back anywhere from approximately 800 B.C. to the A.D. third century. Some people have even argued that certain customs and words of the Native Americans, referred to by some explorers as Indians, show that they had contact at possibly a very early date with Celtic people. If the Celtic settlers visited America at an earlier date, then what happened to them? Did the Celtic settlers merge with the Native Americans who were then existing in the New World?

Legend has it that there were pre-Columbian visits to the New World by early Irish explorers. One of the more interesting claims is that of Ireland's St. Brendan, who lived in the late fifth and early sixth centuries. He was an outstanding sailor and navigator who went on a voyage of exploration with other monks to the Promised Land. The writings about St. Brendan seem to take poetic license, in the way they describe the voyage. Were the stories of St. Brendan's voyage actual descriptions of true events or were they literary creations? Some people argue that it does not matter whether St. Brendan actually traveled to America. The stories of his voyage simply represent the fact that the ancient Irish were skillful seaman, who may have sailed to the New World long before Columbus.

Prince Henry Sinclair, who was Scottish, supposedly set off on a voyage of exploration in approximately 1395, and made several landings in unexplored areas to the west of Scotland. When the prince died in 1404, there was no clear charting of the land that he discovered, so the arguments continue to rage on as to what role, if any, he played in actually discovering what is now known as the New World.

There is a legend that a Welsh prince set off with a fleet of ships for the New World in ancient times. Welsh explorers also have been credited with landing near the area that is now known as Mobile Bay, Alabama, as early as 1170. The major substantiation for this theory is that there was supposedly a tribe of native Americans, known as the Mandans, who lived near the area and showed possible influence by the Welsh. They reportedly included parts of the Welsh language with their own and appeared to physically resemble Europeans. There has even been some argument that archeological finds in the area of Tennessee are similar to forts found in Wales.

Critics of pre-Columbian exploration of America by Europeans argue that sailors did not have the proper technology before the end of the fifteenth century to travel long distances to the New World. Supposedly, ancient sailors could not go over great expanses of water away from the sight of land, because they did not have the ability to handle sails to properly catch the wind and lacked the navigational skills to handle long voyages. It was necessary to have a crew of people large enough to row a ship to its destination. Dependence on rowers for power allegedly kept ships too small for ocean travel. It is reasoned that a small ship could not carry enough food and fresh drinking water to support the rowers on a long trip across a large open expanse of water. This allegedly forced ships before the end of the A.D. fifteenth century to stay within the sight of land for security, to assist in maintaining a course, and to provide access to food and fresh drinking water for their crew. Doubters of early voyages to America, believe it was only when sailors developed adequate navigational skills, learned how to take advantage of sails for power, built ships large enough to provide adequate storage of food and water for a long voyage that it was practical to travel across the oceans.

Did ancient sailors lack the technology to travel across the oceans? The writings of the Roman General Caesar indicate that during his time the Celtic people had the ability to take advantage of the winds for sailing great distances. An ancient type of mechanism called an astrolabe has been found in the ocean. Some researchers believe that the astrolabe may have been used by ancient sailors to navigate courses over vast expanses of water. Could we be underestimating the ability of our ancient ancestors to travel the seas?

It has been argued that some early settlers in the New World did not have to travel completely across the ocean from Europe. These settlers were allegedly from the lost continent of Atlantis which may have been located somewhere in the Atlantic ocean. When Atlantis allegedly sunk the survivors settled in the New World. The lost continent has been credited with providing sophisticated cultural patterns that were accepted by the ancient native inhabitants of the Western Hemisphere. Some people even have taken the position that the legend of Atlantis is based on information about pre-Columbian America brought back by early explorers from Europe. Numerous researchers have indicated there is insufficient evidence to substantiate any connection between pre-Columbian America and any lost continent. Despite widespread interest in the famed Atlantis, many scholars do not believe that there is sufficient proof that it ever actually existed.

Similarities between the ancient Mayans of Central America and the Egyptians have often been cited to prove that there must have been early links between the two civilizations. It has been argued that the Ancient Mayans of America and peoples of the Middle East shared certain economic and religious practices. Could two independent societies in different parts of the world follow similar courses of development without having had contact with one another?

The famous Phoenician traders are another Middle Eastern group who have been credited with exploring America before Columbus. The Phoenicians were great commercial travelers who developed trade far from their native home. They did not, however, keep exact records of where their voyages took them. Possibly, this was because they wanted to keep secret their trade routes so as to secure commercial advantage. It has been argued that they may have traveled all the way around Africa to the New World and traded in the area of the Mayans as early as the sixth century B.C. This would have been approximately two hundred years before Plato wrote his story about the destruction of Atlantis. Could Plato's story of Atlantis have been based upon Phoenician stories of what they had found in the New World?

One piece of evidence that has been introduced to support early travel by Phoenicians to America is a stone found in Brazil in 1872. The inscriptions on it resemble the writings of the language of the Phoenicians. For many years after the stone's discovery it was thought that it was nothing more than a forgery. Some recent scholars have differed from the traditional viewpoint and argued that it was created by ancient pre-Columbian visitors to the area. The language on the stone, supposedly, could not have been forged in the nineteenth century because it was not known to scholars of that time period. Stories have circulated that the Phoenicians and their Hebrew neighbors may have traveled together to the New World to trade. There has been support for the idea that possibly the Phoenicians and ancient Hebrews traveled to America on commercial voyages hundreds of years before the birth of Columbus.

Early explorers from Europe and the Middle East are not the only people who have been credited with visits to the New World before 1492. There may have been voyages across the Pacific to the New World long before even the Vikings set sail on their travels of exploration. Ancient Chinese writings have been interpreted as saying that Chinese monks visited America as early as the A.D. fifth century. Could Chinese explorers have traveled across the Pacific to Mexico or Central America before Columbus?

Researchers have found references to sculpture unearthed in Central America which seemingly resemble Buddhist works of art in China. People from the Pacific Islands have shown tremendous skill in moving from island to island. Some historians believe many of the pacific islands were impacted by ancient migrations of people from Asia. If ancient far eastern people success- fully moved across the Pacific to inhabit the islands, couldn't they have gone even farther to the New World?

The ancestors of Native Americans traveled from Asia over what is now known as the Bering Strait, some 30,000 to 40,000 years ago. There is ample evidence of their early presence in the New World. Weren't the ancient travelers across the Bering Strait the first discovers of America?

If there were other early visitors from the Old World be- fore Columbus, they may have had exchanges with cer- tain tribes of Native Americans. This may explain some of the unique customs and languages of Native Ameri- can tribal groups found in the New World.

The early history of the exploration and cultural de- velopment of America has yet to be fully documented. It appears, however, to be rich in heritage with fascinating secrets possibly yet to be unveiled. No matter what fur- ther research reveals about ancient exploration of the Western Hemisphere, the descendants of the ancient travelers across the Bering Strait should remain a signif- icant factor in pioneering the settlement of the New World. Columbus will continue to be an important his- torical figure because of the great role he played in per- manently opening up America to the rest of the world.

Bibliography

The Lost Dauphin

Doyle, William. *The Oxford History of the French Revolution*. Oxford: Clarendon Press, 1989 (p. 295-296).

Gurney, Gene. *Kingdoms of Europe: An Illustrated Encyclopedia of Ruling Monarchs from Ancient Times to the Present*. New York: Crown Publishers, 1982 (p. 107).

Hardwick, Mollie. *Great Unsolved Mysteries*. Century Books, Ltd., 1984.

Lees, Frederic. *The Dauphin (Louis XVII): The Riddle of the Temple*. Portsmouth, NH: Heinemann, 1922.

Minnigerode, Meade. *The Son of Marie Antoinette: The Mystery of the Temple Tower*. New York: Farrar & Rinehart, Inc., 1934.

Platnick, Kenneth B. *Great Mysteries of History*. New York: Dorset Press, 1971 (p. 89).

The Anastasia Controversy

Kurth, Peter. *Anastasia: The Riddle of Anna Anderson*. Boston: Little, Brown and Company, 1983.

Kurth, Peter. *The Lost World of Nicholas and Alexandra*, Boston: Little, Brown and Company, 1995.

Lincoln, W. Bruce. *The Romanovs: Autocrats of all the Russias*. New York: Anchor Books, Doubleday, 1981.

Mackenzie, F. A. *World Famous Crimes*. Geoffrey Bles, 1927 (p. 109).

Massie, Robert K. *Nicholas and Alexandra*. New York: Atheneum, 1967.

Massie, Robert K. *The Romanovs: The Final Chapter*. New York: Random House, 1995.

Moynahan, Brian. *The Russian Century*. New York: Random House, 1994.

Platnick, Kenneth B. *Great Mysteries of History*. New York: Dorset Press, 1987 (p. 105).

Radzinsky, Edvard. *The Last Tsar: The Life and Death of Nicholas II*. New York: Doubleday, 1992.

Richards, Guy. *The Hunt for the Czar*. Garden City, NY: Doubleday, 1970.

Summers, Anthony, and Tom Mangold. *The File on the Tsar*. Centerport, NY: Fontana Books, 1976.

The Missing English Princes

Cannon, John, and Ralph Griffiths. *The Oxford Illustrated History of the British Monarchy*. Oxford: Oxford University Press, 1988.

The Complete Works of William Shakespeare. Amaranth Press, 1921; Cambridge: Cambridge University Press, 1921; London: Henneruod Publications, Ltd., 1982; London: Octopus Books, Ltd., 1985.

Griffiths, Ralph A., and Roger S. Thomas. *The Making of the Tudor Dynasty*. New York: St. Martin's Press, 1985.

Gurney, Gene. *Kingdoms of Europe: An Illustrated Encyclopedia of Ruling Monarchs from Ancient Times to the Present*. New York: Crown Publishers, Inc., 1982.

Kendall, Paul Murray. *Richard the Third*. New York: W. W. Norton Company, Inc., 1955.

Plowden, Alison. *The House of Tudor*. New York: Stein and Day, 1976.

Reader's Digest Association. *Quest for the Past*. Pleasantville, New York and Montreal: Reader's Digest Association, 1984 (p. 303-305).

Ross, Charles. *English Monarchs: Richard III*. Berkeley and Los Angeles: University of California Press, 1981.

Rowse, A. L. *The Tower of London in the History of England*. New York: G. P. Putnam's Sons, 1972 (p. 25).

St. Aubyn, Giles. *The Year of Three Kings*. New York: Atheneum, 1983.

Seward, Desmond. *Richard III: England's Black Legend*. New York: Franklin Watts, 1983.

Simon, Lisa. *Of Virtue Rare: Margaret Beaufort, Matriarch of the House of Tudor*. Boston: Houghton Mifflin Co., 1982.

The True Identity of Prisoner Number 7 — Rudolf Hess

Aymar, Brandt, and Edward Sagarin. *A Pictorial History of the World's Great Trials from Socrates to Jean Harris*. New York: Bonanza Books, 1967 (p. 301).

Bird, Eugene K. *Prisoner #7, Rudolf Hess: The Thirty Years in Jail of Hitler's Deputy Fuhrer*. New York: Viking Press, 1974.

Fishman, Jack. *Long Knives and Short Memories: Lives and Crimes of the 7 Nazi: The Spandau Prison Story*. New York: Richardson & Steirman Book Publishers, 1986.

Haswell, Jock. *Murders and Mysteries*. Futura Publications, 1987 (p. 134-143).

Schwarzwaller, Wulf. *Rudolph Hess, The Last Nazi*. Bethesda, MD: National Press Books, Inc., 1988.

Speer, Albert. *Inside the Third Reich*. New York: Macmillan Company, 1970.

The Man in the Iron Mask

Dumas, Alexandre. *The Man in the Iron Mask*. Laurel, NY: Lightyear Press, 1982.

Godwin, John. *This Baffling World*. New York: Hart Publishing Company, Inc., 1968 (p. 121).

Gurney, Gene. *Kingdoms of Europe: An Illustrated Encyclopedia of Ruling Monarchs from Ancient Times to the Present*. New York: Crown Publishing, Inc., 1982 (p. 99).

Noone, John. *The Man Behind the Iron Mask*. New York: St. Martin's Press, 1988.

Platnick, Kenneth B. *Great Mysteries of History*. New York: Dorset Press, 1971 (p. 75).

Was There a Robin Hood?

Ebbutt, M. I. *The British: Myths and Legends*. London: Braken Books, 1985 (p. 314).

Holt, Robin. *Robin Hood*. London: Thames and Hudson, Ltd., 1982.

Gilbert, Henry. *Robin Hood and the Men of the Greenwood*. London: Braken Books, 1985.

Mystery, Intrigue & Suspense. London: Octopus Books Limited, 1987.

Scott, *Sir Walter. Ivanhoe*. Heron Books, 1819 (p. 311).

The Czar's Empty Coffin

Dzlewanowski, M. K. *Alexander I: Russian's Mysterious Tsar*. New York: Hippocrene Books, 1990.

Hingley, Ronald. *The Tsars 1533-1917*. Vol H-947. New York: Macmillan, 1968.

Lincoln, W. Bruce. *The Romanovs: Autocrats of all the Russias*. New York: Anchor Books, Doubleday, 1981.

Platnick, Kenneth B. *Great Mysteries of History*. New York: Dorset Press, 1971 (p. 127).

Troyat, Henri. *Alexander of Russia—Napoleon's Conqueror*. Translated by Joan Pinkham. New York: E. P. Putton, Inc., 1980 (p. 300-304).

Was There a King Arthur?

American Heritage Books. *Discovery of Lost Worlds*. New York: American Heritage Books, 174 and 194.

Ashe, Geoffrey, in association with Debrett's Peerage. *The Discovery of King Arthur*. New York: Owl Books, Henry Holt and Company, 1985.

Ebbuitt, M. I. *The British: Myth and Legends*. London: Braken Books, 1985 (p. 265).

Edge, David, and John Miles Paddock. *Arms and Armor of the Medieval Knight: An Illustrated History of Weaponry in the Middle Ages*. England: Crescent Books, 1988.

Gilbery, Henry. *King Arthur's Knights*. London: Braken Books, 1985.

Goodrich, Norma Lorre. *King Arthur*. New York: Harper & Row, 1986.

Goodrich, Norma Lorre. *Merlin*. New York: Harper & Row, 1988.

Jenkins, Elizabeth. *The Mystery of King Arthur*. New York: Dorset Press, 1975.

Jackson, Robert, and Patrick Stephans. *Dark Age Britain: What to See and Where*. Cambridge: Cambridge Press, 1984.

Malory, Sir Thomas. *Le Morte D'Arthur*. New Hyde Park, NY: University Books, Inc., 1961.

Malory, Sir Thomas. *Le Morte D'Arthur*. Modernized as to spelling and punctuation by A. W. Pollard, 1955.

Matthews, John, and Robert John Stewart. *Warriors of Arthur*. New York: Blandford Press, 1987.

Rolleston, T. W. *Celtic: Myths and Legends*. London: Braken Books, 1986 (p. 336).

Wilson, Jan. *Undiscovered*. New York: Beech Tree Books, 1987 (p. 73).

Who Discovered America?

Blegen, Theodore C. *The Kensington Rune Stone: New Light on an Old Riddle*. St. Paul, MN: Minnesota Historical Society.

Boorstin, Daniel J. *The Discoverers*. New York: Random House, 1983.

Casson, Lionel, Robert Claiborne, Brian Fagan, and Walter Karp. *Mysteries of the Past: Who First Crossed the Ocean?* New York: American Heritage Press, 1977.

Cumming, W. P., R. A. Skelton, and D. B. Quinn. *The Discovery of North America*. New York: American Heritage Press, 1971.

Cumming, W.P., R.A. Skelton, and D.B. Quinn. *Discovery of Lost Worlds*. New York: American Heritage Press, 1979 (p. 222).

Enterline, James Robert. *Viking America: The Norse Crossings and Their Legacy.* New York: Doubleday, 1972.

Fagan, Brian. *New Treasures of the Past.* New York: Barrons, 1987 (p. 38, 82, 86).

Fell, Barry. *America B.C..* New York: New York Times Book Co., 1976.

Fell, Barry. *Bronze Age America.* Boston: Little, Brown and Company, 1982.

Gordon, Cyrus H. *Riddles in History.* New York: Crown Publishers, Inc., 1974.

Haening, Peter. *Ancient Mysteries.* Australia: Peter Haening and Sidgwick & Jackson Hutchinson of Australia, 1977 (p. 45, 56, 57).

Hibben, Frank C. *The Lost Americans—The Story of the Man They Said Never Was: Old Stone-Age American.* New York: Thomas Y. Crowell Co., 1946.

Holand, Tjalmar, R. *Exploration in America before Columbus.* New York: Twayne Publishers, Inc., 1956.

Kelley, Charles J., Campbell W. Pennington, and Robert L. Rands. *Man Across the Sea. Problems of Pre-Columbian Contacts.* Austin, TX: University of Texas Press, 1971.

Norman, Bruce. *Footsteps.* Topsfield, MA: Salem House Publishers, 1987 (p. 195).

Platnick, Kenneth B. *Great Mysteries of History.* New York: Dorset Press, 1987 (p. 105).

Reader's Digest Association. *The World's Last Mysteries.* Pleasantville, NY and Montreal: Reader's Digest Association, Inc., 1976 (p. 50).

Wilbur, Keith C. *Early Explorers of North America.* Old Saybrook, CT: The Globe Pequot Press, 1989.

About the Author

Fred Neff has had a life long interest in history and the law. From the time he was a young boy he has taken a special interest in studying true life criminal cases. As a part of his early interest in true crime mysteries Mr. Neff has made an extensive study of criminology, historical research methods and law enforcement investigation techniques.

Fred Neff graduated in 1970 from the University of Minnesota College of Education with High Distinction. He taught social studies in the Hopkins School system. He introduced the study of historical mysteries to his students to enhance their knowledge of the past and their problem-solving skills. The reception was so positive in his first year of teaching that the University of Minnesota assigned student teachers to Fred, so that they would be exposed to his teaching techniques. From 1972-1976 he attended William Mitchell College of Law. While attending law school he taught at the University of Minnesota, University of Wisconsin and Inver Hills College.

After graduating from law school in 1976 he served as a criminal prosecutor. Subsequently, he left public service as a prosecutor and was appointed to do criminal defense work for the Public Defenders Conflict Panel and Juvenile Justice Panel. He has also acted as private counsel on numerous criminal cases. As a part of his work as a lawyer he has dealt with extensive criminal investigations. Mr. Neff has taught classes for lawyers, legal personnel and law enforcement officers in handling criminal cases. He has also served as a legal advisor to peace officers and private investigators.

Mr. Neff's experience and knowledge in the field of legal matters has led to his election and appointment as a member of the board of directors of a number of organizations including a national insurance company. In 1989, Mr. Neff acted as a co-host on a television program Great Puzzles in History. Each program covered a different historical mystery. The show was very popular and ran continually from 1989-1991.

He has received many awards for his accomplishments and community involvement including the city of St. Paul Citizen of the Month Award in 1975, a Commendation for Distinguished Service from the Sibley County Attorney's office in 1980, the WCCO Good Neighbor Award in 1985, the HLS Justice Award in 1985, the Lamp of Knowledge award from the Twin Cities Lawyers Guild in 1986, commendation awards from N.W. Community T.V. 1989, 1990, and 1991, and the Presidential Medal of Merit Award from President George Bush in 1990.